CLUTCH

MACHETE

Joy Castro and Rachel Cochran, Series Editors

# CLUTCH

## AN EDUCATION AT WORK

Linda Pawlenty

MAD CREEK BOOKS, AN IMPRINT OF
THE OHIO STATE UNIVERSITY PRESS
COLUMBUS

Copyright © 2025 by Linda Pawlenty.
All rights reserved.
Published by Mad Creek Books, an imprint of The Ohio State University Press.

Library of Congress Cataloging-in-Publication Data

Cover design by Brad Norr
Text design by Stuart Rodriguez
Type set in Adobe Caslon and Rockwell

∞ The paper used in this publication meets the minimum requirements of the American National Standard for Information Sciences—Permanence of Paper for Printed Library Materials. ANSI Z39.48-1992.

*For my fellow drivers, my comrades,
and for those doing the work*

This is a special dedication to Bob Finley.

Bob and I had been together for two years when, on July 11, 2024, a motorist turned in front of his motorcycle on the highway. My Bob died, they say, instantly.

On July 11, 2024, this book had already been written. I had turned in copyedits less than two weeks before. We were about to begin all the fun stuff that goes along with book publication: cover design, seeing the proofs, planning a book launch. And then.

When the bulk of this book was written, Bob wasn't yet a part of my intimate life. Six months before I graduated with my PhD he was hired as a truck driver where I worked. Later Bob told me I was a frustrating person for these six months because I was "always reading in my truck." Hopeful, he waited. When I finally quit studying and emerged out of that truck cab, Bob and I became inseparable.

You'll see Bob appear in this text as himself, as he wanted to be. The Bob in the book is my Bob.

My Bob is the reason this book was finished. He encouraged me to meet for coffee with my mentor, tracked down my future editor at the writing conference in Seattle, was patient and kind as I fretted over the final manuscript submission. It was his funny and creative brain that invented many of the pseudonyms we used for our concrete world. When Bob died, I stopped caring about publishing the book because I stopped caring about everything.

But. He told everyone he could that I was a published author, even before I was. It was his excitement, his pride in me, his unequivocal love.

I had to keep going, have to, because Bob wanted to see this book. It is because of Bob that you have it in your hands.

So that's what I want you to know about Bob Finley. His love, his excitement, his dedication, his care, his joy.

My dear Bob, I love you. Thank you for holding my hand. Thank you for never letting go.

# Contents

## PREFACE

| | |
|---|---|
| Dawning | xv |
| Some Crazy Tom Potter Shit | xvii |

## ESSAYS

| | |
|---|---|
| Navigating | 3 |
| Definitions | 7 |
| Cite Your Work | 10 |
| A Truck Driver Is Born | 13 |
| Feedback | 24 |
| Rules and Regs | 25 |
| Sharing | 33 |
| My Pretty Eyes | 35 |
| Truth and Beauty | 57 |
| Participation | 59 |
| And Yet Another Instance Where a Word Wields Its Power | 61 |
| Please | 74 |
| Legal Protection | 75 |
| I Was Talking to Bob and Said: | 84 |
| Assets | 85 |

| | |
|---|---|
| Conviviality | 96 |
| ¿Pero dónde están los hispanos? | 97 |
| Refrain | 110 |
| Schooled | 111 |
| Not a Chick | 122 |
| Partnership | 127 |
| Craft | 128 |
| What We Might Do | 132 |
| Parts of Speech | 134 |
| Uniform | 136 |
| Mouse | 160 |
| Lacking | 161 |
| Talking Back | 168 |
| Blindside | 171 |
| Refuge | 185 |

## EPILOGUE

| | |
|---|---|
| Why I Write | 193 |
| | |
| Acknowledgments | 197 |
| Notes | 199 |
| Further Reading | 207 |

This is a work of creative nonfiction. Events are written here as I remember them. With few exceptions, names of people and businesses, and perhaps some identifying characteristics, have been changed.

# PREFACE

# Dawning

It is that hour, the sun dawning a speckle of pink in the east and I breathe in the gift of being awake to it, standing in the parking lot with my head thrown back to the sky, searching for stars, marveling, gaping at the bright white fuzz of the moon. I bend the silver handle and the door of my truck cab clicks open; I climb up and inside and pull it shut behind me, safe, powerful. This is a home. A long, strong silent row of machines begins to buzz and utters a guttural purr as one by one, we drivers arrive for the day and take our dutiful places. To see each other in the darkness of dawn is intimate. It is best though, when I am there before all this bustle, and the heavy silence, the peace and incongruity of standing in a concrete wasteland but being able to hear birds trill and whistle, joy and beauty, it is best when that silence and dark amplifies the massive heavy bodies of our trucks and I feel more where I am. Every part of my truck has a different texture, and I run my hand across these parts and sense the bigness of what I am doing, not hauling concrete but becoming a part of this giant as we prepare to move together across and through the city, into its green spaces and most intimate recesses of alleyways and history. Fantastical because there are others beside me doing it too, one unit although we are so individual. There are simply so many men here in this alternate reality where inexplicably 99 percent of the women have vanished. Men here with me my fellow drivers, yes, my compadres my brothers my little brothers my uncles my nemesis my I adore you or you drive me crazy depending on the day. Yes, those men, but also so many men, so many men at jobsites, the contractors customers clientes whatever you want to call them, at this place and that place and that place and that one, there is never any doubt what I will find because it is a certainty there are just men, everywhere, and I am used to it and I am not.

But more importantly. There is the driving, this truck, my truck this force of a natural home more mine than the one where I lay my head. The driving is a beautiful thing and me in that truck is a beautiful thing and so are the concrete jobs, where I can be a blessing to the men there or I can wreak havoc, though I don't, because it too is beautiful to do work with others and to share the stress and the sweat and the danger and the laughing and the love that those small moments beget when you are all there fighting for the same damn thing.

# Some Crazy Tom Potter Shit

I eased my truck to the top of the hill and stopped. Looking down, you had to stop. I pondered whether I was an idiot or the best damn truck driver on the planet. I took a huge breath. I took another. I said a prayer. I eased out the clutch and began the descent.

My concrete truck, truck number 138, shivered a little as I transitioned from clutch and brake and we went slowly down. So slowly. My truck's rigid frame curved over the top of the hill and we were parallel with its slope, his nose pointed at the bottom. We were so tall, and top heavy, juggling a giant spinning drum of concrete twisting through the air, the center of gravity so high, gravity, gravity. The path was narrow, with little room between the house and the opposite edge, where the dirt fell away, where a misplaced tire would slip then fall, everything tipping, and then—don't imagine it—gravity, the gravity.

We weren't alone. The bent old man was near the bottom of the hill, moving more and faster than I had ever seen him move. Eyes on me and 138, on the tires and the earth, were they straight and would it hold, hands in front of him with palms face to face, rotating at the wrists, the sign to keep it straight, keep it straight. We eased on down. Time stopped.

All eyes were on us, which was a giveaway that the men were nervous, which was a giveaway that this was not something every driver would do. We were doing it.

138 creaked and groaned and popped, but I had control and we were doing it. Hug the house, close as we could, keep away from that other edge. We'd be fine.

As we reached the bottom the old man started pointing to my left, *just miss the corner of the house with your mirror,* he had said, I remembered. This was the dangerous part, turning a little while on a hill, you always went down a hill straight, always, never on a diagonal with that drum spinning so high, the fins inside of it lifting that concrete up before it fell gloriously, mixing, mixing, keep it moving. I just missed the corner of the house with the mirror and we had done it, the sudden rush of bodies I sensed as the men let out their breath and scampered from where they had been watching, the worst over, *she did it.*

There was no room to turn around behind this house. We nosed up to the adjacent yard as much as we could, 138 and I, wiggling the tail end around to the patio. It would be enough. I pulled on the air brakes, and 138 hissed with relief, stock still, and I breathed with him.

We were there.

# ESSAYS

# **Navigating**

This is a book about trucks and work and books and schooling, because those are the things that made me, make me, and to take any one away is to blur the rest, to alter, be dishonest, break me.

This is also a book about power.

And this is a book about how I navigate separate worlds as a PhD in academia and in my job as a truck driver in the construction industry. Within those seemingly separate spheres, trucking and the university, there is still more division. Gendered worlds, classed worlds, worlds divided by language, by bodies, and united by all of this too.

My identity is stitched together from incongruous pieces, parts complex and misperceived. To be to be working class, to be "educated": but the words are wrong, they cut, they wound, they go deep but not deep enough. Regardless of how I name these parts: here I am. I exist, with a foot firmly in each land. And yet living with a border running underneath me does not feel stable, does not allow me to be at ease. This border between classes and peoples, expectations and comforts, languages and movements.

How do I navigate that?
How does anyone?

I move differently. Not like the men, or like the women, like the drivers or the professors. But I am happy with my walk. That it is different. That it is powerful. I am powerful. I have solid self-assurance that the people I work alongside each day, the people who physically labor, my people, deserve better than what we get from the people that employ us, the people making laws, the people molding curriculum. Even with this unwavering belief, there are moments when I am swallowed by doubt and loss of hope and the exhaustion of knowing we'll always be fighting the shitty types of people and power in this world.

So this book is about that power, that larger-than-life force that bears down on us and compels us to question the course we've charted or the one we've dreamed of. It is about the forms power takes, in the life of an academic and a truck driver: the power of machines and the bodies that drive them, the power of gender, of the academy and middle management. The power of language, of education and labor, of sabotage and resistance, of class. It is about the power to resist the conditioning to do what we've been told to and to hold our tongues.

This book is about the long road to get to that place of resistance.

•

A PhD and a truck driver walk into a bar.

Kidding. I'll cut the jokes.

For each of these identities, the labor required of the mind is different, and the labor required of the body is different. The physical environment is different, the people that surround me, the norms governing behavior—different. I can, in some ways, leave being a truck driver at the door when I come home; on the other hand, the manual labor marks me in a way being an academic does not. As a graduate student, my work followed me every day, in the form of emails from students and my department and in the pressures to read, write, and question. My role as a student left no visible sign on my body (at least not to middle-class viewers), although it did wear it down from fatigue in a similar way that driving does. This is my story of going back and forth between these two selves. Although I am no longer a graduate student—I am now a PhD, una doctora, a writer—the distinction between two halves remains. This story is for those of us who cannot, or who choose not to, leave manual labor behind. For the children and partners of working people, whose family lives are marked by the work of parents and relatives, the firsts of generations who are navigating a sea uncharted and unknown by the people closest to them. Manual labor matters—and deserves a place in our everyday conversations—because it is a part of the lives of so many of the living, breathing humans sitting next to us or in front of us in the classroom, or in the line behind us at the grocery store, or cleaning our offices, or outside replacing our sidewalks. But maybe you know this already, because it's a part of you, and you're searching for others who know it too. Physical labor matters because people matter, because nothing we benefit from each day has been untouched by someone's laboring hands.

What I also recognize, from this place in between that I inhabit, are the privileges I am afforded. I am an Anglo/white person living in Lincoln, Nebraska. I am a recently graduated PhD who held a fully funded graduate position at a research university. I have no debt. I am a native speaker of English, which in this country also grants me power. I identify as female: here my power or lack of it depends on the context. Regardless, I have a knapsack full of privileges free for the using. There are times, many times, when I encounter conflict, when my identity is challenged, when I am othered, when I am made to feel as though my voice, my body, my heart—none of it matters. I am othered because of my professions, my gender, my way of speaking. Yet I hold enough privilege to walk away from much of this if I choose, to hide from it maybe, which is a privilege not afforded to everyone.

I can't answer the question of why I came to truck driving, but this was the driving force (pun not intended, but come on) behind the ways in which I orient myself here, now. My role as a driver has led me to people with economic, cultural, and linguistic backgrounds different from mine, and these working roles have blended into personal relationships. Because of these, I now tread different waters than I ever imagined I would. My entry point into language was through work, my real entry point into my university studies was through work, and my consciousness about these things arose through the intersections of graduate school and work. I do not claim to speak for anyone other than myself, and at times, I am not even sure of what I want to say. I am thinking about my own place in the journey, constantly, about the journeys of others, and about what spaces we share and what spaces we will never be able to share.

# Definitions

When I was much younger and still in the beginnings of my trucking life, I had a job where my customers were farmers in the beef and dairy industries. I drove this heavy-ass semi-truck (almost 95,000 pounds) chock full of cattle food to feedlots and dairies across Nebraska and Kansas. *Sir* was a common word in my vocabulary, and I'd reflexively invoke it often whenever I talked to the men who owned and ran these places.

"It's not 'sir,' don't bother with that," they'd say to me. "I work for a living."

"Well, that's all the more reason for me to call you that," I'd reply, believing that *sir* was a term of respect. I never used the word for someone I disliked unless it was sarcastic.

It took me years to figure out that to these farmers *sir* meant something different than what I intended. Of course they worked for a living, most of us do, but they considered the work they did *real* work, and the work others did, the *sirs* of the world, something quite different. A *sir*, as best I could hypothesize, was a suit-and-tie guy who sat behind a desk all day, never getting his hands dirty. A farmer, as I think these customers saw it, had "dirty hands, clean money." A *sir* had just the opposite.

The way work is defined depends mightily on who is doing the defining, and those definitions are laden with cultural—and often deeply personal—significance to those that use them. So defining work, like so many other things, isn't straightforward: understanding what it is and what it means is like driving through a commercial construction site, absolutely rife with hazards: rebar poking out of the ground, ready to gouge a tire. People darting around the truck, careless and not watching. Cranes working overhead. Someone hitting a natural gas line. Holes in the ground, really big holes. Things falling. Obstacles everywhere. No matter how careful you are, safety is never guaranteed.

When I talk about work and labor here, I am thinking about specific things, although I know others use these terms differently. I use *work* here in the way Mike Rose defines it: "purposeful, remunerated effort that provides goods or services for another." When the word *labor* slips into my vocabulary, I mean the same thing.

And when I talk about work and labor, I refer to what would, in most instances in English, be thought of as blue-collar jobs (another troubling term, because of its gendered nature): construction and truck driving, shift work, cleaning, waiting tables, and so on. I am thinking of work associated with physicality and/or with working-class status (this isn't without problem, either, since working class also lacks a uniform definition).

I do this while acknowledging there are many other types of labor and work, both paid and unpaid, some of which overlap these professions: for example, there is the common term intellectual labor, which I believe is part and parcel of blue-collar work, although intellectual labor is often used, for example, to describe the work of an academic. And then there is emotional and spiritual labor, labor as in the act of giving birth, and so on. Because it would be, well, laborious to include such specificity each time I need to say labor or work, my use here assumes association with job, career, and class status for simplicity's sake, not to ignore the many other types of labor that exist.

# Cite Your Work

I saw my father working when I was a child, coming home in his Air Force fatigues, and later, after Air Force retirement, remember him being gone overnight driving that school bus, shuffling buses between cities. I saw my mother attend night school for her bachelor's degree; my brother and I attended class with her once or twice—what else to do with us? I can still see the classroom, us sitting near the back, feel the specialness of being permitted to be there. Later, in her first years as a fifth-grade teacher, my hand cramping from so much time folded into a pair of scissors, carefully cutting construction paper shapes—round caterpillar bodies, wavy scoops of ice cream—to be used by my mother's students.

These memories are flashes, images, a single scene, and so I think that's how it was in childhood, the work of my parents cropping up now and then in flashes, present of course but subtly. Work was not in our faces, not rolled out as destiny.

But neither was college. For children whose parents don't go to college, or who fight their way through a nontraditional route (whose tradition is it, anyway?), college is as much a mystery as anything else. I entered both college and work from a sort of limbo space and had to fake it 'til I made it once I got there. My parents had no idea what I was doing. I had no idea what I was doing. Which is how I found mentors, or how they found me.

In trucking there was Dennis, almost old enough to be my grandfather, 5′4″ and a fighter, no one imagining we'd bond. I followed him down so many highways in one of my first trucking jobs, especially in winter, learning from him how fast was just right, what the truck could handle, how not to be afraid.

Before Dennis there was Kat, my trainer at my very first trucking job, kind, generous, smart and strong and beyond patient, giving me every opportunity that she could to practice backing up a trailer, not angry when I missed a turn during a foggy night in Missouri and drove over an hour past the correct highway, buying me a meal when I'd help her unload our dollar-store freight. Dr. J and Dr. Darcy during my early English days, trying to get my bachelor's. They let me be me and shaped the thinker I became.

But.

Everyone was in their separate spheres. No one crossed over. Dennis and Kat and my truckers there, my professors here.

And in those separate worlds, I'm never quite right, never the expert, always at least a little bit on the outside. I speak as a woman in a truck and am ignored, a man voices the same idea and is heralded as an experienced pro. I speak as a truck driver in the classroom and am a novelty, a peer voices the same idea but cites that famous French critic and is praised as a keen reader. Linda Hogan, a writer and member of the Chickasaw Nation, writes about the difficult and lonely process of "education":

> When I say that I spent my life in self-education, I want people to know that part of this was done even when I went to college.... There were no classes that made any connection

to my own life experience or perception of the world. The closest I came to learning what I needed was in a course on labor literature, and the lesson there was in knowing that there were writers who lived similar lives to ours.

This is one of the ways that higher education perpetuates racism and classism. By ignoring our lives and work, by creating standards for only their work.

Hogan, I, and countless others find ourselves forced to justify our way of doing the work. Speaking with our unfiltered voices is labeled a radical action, and Hogan asks, "Why is it that telling our lives is a subversive thing to do?" Why do people demand corroboration before they buy the story, whether it's in the form of a coworker's agreement or the words of the ubiquitously cited theorists? So I am not using my own experience to support the theory, no. My experience *is* the theory. It is supported by what others have connected, contextualized, made clearer. But it also IS.

Let's be subversive. Be fucking radical.
Let's fight to be.

# A Truck Driver Is Born

Growing up, if I had been asked to categorize my family, I would have described us as a middle class, "typical" midwestern family: one mom, one dad, one daughter, one son. My brother and I never wanted for anything material: food, shelter, toys, experiences, the freedom to go to any college that accepted us (not because we had the disposable income for college, but because my parents assured us they would "figure it out"). I had close friends with more siblings or with single parents, and I saw Angie, Natalie, and Diane go without many of the luxuries I enjoyed. Comparing myself to my friends is what formed my definition of middle class.

While in some ways that's probably accurate enough, I now see nuance. My mother and father were careful not to let us relive their childhoods. My father, born in 1944 in rural Minnesota, never throws anything away and has told us more than once that his scrupulous saving is not because he enjoys being thrifty, but because, growing up, his family was poor. My mother teased him about being a penny pincher, but my dad is the reason I am doing okay today.

I cut coupons.

I wash out plastic freezer bags to reuse them.

Do my own oil changes, brake changes, minor truck repairs.

Save the pennies, Dad said, and you don't have to watch the dollars. I am proud of my thrift (and I think he is too).

There was never a question that my brother and I would attend college. It was not put to us as an option, nor did it feel forced. This was a product of my parents' careful design. My father, like his older brothers, entered the military when he was old enough, and spent twenty-seven years in the Air Force, earning an associate's degree in avionic systems technology from the Community College of the Air Force in 1991. This was just six months before his retirement. When I asked why he completed his degree so close to the end of his career, my father said laughing: "Because I was working on that thing a long time and wasn't too much interested in getting it." My mother also enlisted in the Air Force when young, leaving after serving the minimum four years, presumably to have me. As a mother in her late thirties she decided to become a teacher, earned a bachelor's degree in education, and when I was twenty or so, a master's degree. She taught elementary school until her retirement.

So go to college I did. It was a tortured path to find the right major and department, hell, even the right school. Dead set on fleeing Nebraska, I spent two years at a New York university before I discovered I was too shy to be a photojournalist. Back to Nebraska I went. Next came a year working in the parts department of a Volkswagen/Audi/Mazda/Porsche dealership. Then some community college courses to prepare for a career in nursing, and a switch to a pre-med track before organic chemistry did me in. Eventually someone set me straight. An insightful English professor said to me, "Why don't you give English a try?" He pointed me toward the path that would change my life. I had found my way at the University of Nebraska Omaha (UNO), fifteen minutes from my father's house (my parents had since divorced). I set my sights on becoming a professor of English literature. I didn't want so much to teach, I think, as to simply live in a world of books. It seemed that getting a PhD and teaching was the best way to do that.

After changing my mind so many times, I had been in school for what felt like ages. At the completion of my bachelor of arts, I was twenty-five years old and living in my father's house, with plans to enroll in graduate school after a year off. But I had a very specific plan for that year, and it wasn't backpacking around Europe or taking an extended party trip to Mexico.

I wanted to work. I wanted to be a truck driver.

•

And what do you think my parents thought? Goodness only knows. My father claims he really can't remember how he felt when the daughter he raised so carefully announced she wanted to be a truck driver. Here I was, finally about to graduate college, with a solid future job as a professor in mind, and I had to go and come up with this. A truck driver. Of all things.

There is no obvious trail of breadcrumbs that would make this decision seem logical. The most common question I am asked today is, "What made you want to drive a truck?," but this is something I don't have a satisfying answer for, or rather, an answer that satisfies others. I pause and stare at my questioner, or look at the ground, or sigh. On the long-running television reality series *Ice Road Truckers*, the show's first featured female driver, Lisa Kelly, describes her reason for becoming a truck driver as such: "Because I wanted to—I became a trucker because I wanted to." I've always thought she said it best. This should be enough. And yet, people demand an explanation. But I am telling you, in print:

No, I had no relatives that were truck drivers and I didn't know anyone that did the job.

No, I didn't grow up on a farm driving other equipment, wasn't around trucks.

Nope, I wasn't a so-called gearhead into cars and other machines.

I just wanted to.

*Ice Road Truckers* debuted on the History Channel in the early 2000s, but at time of my decision I had never seen the show, so no pop culture model led me to trucking. I was just an awkward young woman who loved to read and dream. My closest experiences with trucks involved childhood vacations, when my brother and I would wave at the truck drivers as our family's hulking gray conversion van, Betsy, lumbered by on the interstates, us kids begging the drivers to honk their air horns, delighted beyond measure when they complied. That, and only that, was my history with trucking.

But if I am still pressed for an explanation, well. I realize that at the time there were frequent commercials on TV for a local, private truck driving school called JTL. Maybe simply seeing these doesn't explain my choice, but it does explain how I transitioned quickly from an English undergrad to an over-the-road driver. I was going to do it! But just for a year, just until I started graduate school. I guess this was my gap year, after all.

A month before graduation, I had already enrolled myself in truck driving school. I sat at my desk in my pretty purple bedroom on the top floor of my father's house and nervously picked up the phone. Shelly, the extremely nice woman who owned the school with her husband Dave, told me the cost of enrollment at JTL was $4,040 dollars. $4,000 was for the tuition, and $40 for the books.

Wow. Okay.

I know what you're thinking. There are books for truck driving school? Indeed: the 2007 edition of the Rand McNally Motor

Carriers' Road Atlas, and the "green book," otherwise known as the Federal Motor Carrier Safety Administration's regulations (or the FMCSR), both indispensable tools for every commercial driver.

Or maybe you are reeling at the tuition. I don't remember if I was. I probably had what many middle-class, Catholic school, suburban white kids had: a taken-for-granted confidence that my parents would somehow see me through.

Because really, I worked part-time at the Home Depot and didn't have that kind of money, so I did what any kid (or, ehm, adult: I was twenty-five) might do in that situation. I asked my dad for the money. I asked for a loan, promising to pay him back after getting a job as a real, live, truck driver.

We were standing in his kitchen when he handed me a check. "Okay," said Dad. "I just hope you do this for more than a month."

With that vote of confidence, I sent in the check for $4,040 to Shelly, finished my bachelor's degree and graduated with my parents, my brother, and Angie cheering me across the stage, and then anxiously awaited the first day of an entirely different educational experience. Neither myself nor my father knew that the moment in the kitchen would completely alter my future, my entire sense of self. I was prepared to drive for a year and then dedicate my life to serious study as an academic, (although what that meant was fuzzy, only imagined), but what happened instead is a much better story, one I had never dreamed in all that time I had spent in books.

Only now, writing this, do I understand why: because I never saw a life like this lived in books; it simply was not present in anything I had read.

•

I was a spectacular success in truck driving school. I passed at the top of the class. I was hired at Werner Enterprises, a huge national transportation company based in Omaha, worked there for a few months, hated it, then went to drive for a small outfit in the small town of Blair, Nebraska. Three years later, I hesitantly took an office job at an international agriculture company, where I would work in a brown cubicle in a brown building for more than five years, still unbelievable to me even as I type it now. But that ugly cubicle allowed me to spend my nights back at UNO, class by class chipping away at a master's degree in English.

It took me five years to earn my master's; for a traditional student it might have taken two. The closer I got to a degree, the more I could smell freedom from the cubicle, which I had begun to hate with a passion previously unknown to me. I dreaded going into that office every day. I opened my eyes each morning and felt a crushing gloom at the thought of my job before I had even risen from bed. I would arrive at the crisp, new, well-maintained office building, push open the two security doors, see the brown carpet, and my mood would plummet still lower, wondering how I would make it through the next eight hours.

So I was beside myself with anticipation as I neared graduation with my master's degree. I was elated when I was selected to be the graduate speaker at my college's graduation ceremony, and it was my writing skills and my (at that time) brief trucking career that helped me achieve this. I called my graduate speech "Of Books and Big Rigs: A Woman's Journey through Education." Behind the podium, my leg was shaking like a dog's hind leg—nerves—but I delivered the lines I knew by heart almost flawlessly, to thousands of students and their families, and to my family in the audience, stage left. A thank you letter from the dean later that month said that, in a survey done after the event, one enthusiastic graduate commenting on the speeches referred to me as "the English Master Trucker." It would have been tough to knock me from the cloud I was on.

•

A month after that graduation, I sat in an almost empty classroom at the community college. It was just me and several other job-fair hopefuls. A master's qualified me to teach English, so here I sat, sweaty, nervous, and ready to be interviewed.

Applicants came and went into an adjoining room where various college deans sat at all these different tables. I was still waiting when the door popped open and a lonely looking guy poked his head into the room. "Hi, everyone," he said. "I'm the Dean of Applied Technology, and if anyone is waiting to talk with me, I'm available."

Applied Technology? My gears started to turn. Pretty sure this place has a truck driving school . . . I wonder . . . I got up and walked to the door, told the nice lady outside of it I wanted to speak to that Dean. Why not? I was there as an English applicant, but I was also a truck driver. Would I be qualified to teach at that school?

I was soon seated across from this man, a quiet, approachable guy with a long face, glasses, graying hair, and a bland suit. He started talking to me about the length of the driving school program, about the cost. Wait, what? "Oh—no, I'm sorry." I interrupted him. "I already have a CDL. I wanted to know if I had the qualifications to teach truck driving?"

He stared at me, trying to process this. "Oh!" He collected himself. "I'm sorry, I just assumed . . ."

I smiled. Frustrating as it was to be stereotyped, I also enjoyed surprising people and watching them try to regain their footing.

I explained the experience I had and told him about my master's degree for good measure. He took my information, and I went back to the other classroom to wait for the English dean. That interview had less surprises and also went well, but there was a waiting list for English teachers, supply exceeding demand. It would be months before I got a call back from the English department for a formal interview. But a few days after the job fair, my phone rang. I was sitting in my sad brown and beige cubicle when it happened. The head instructor for the truck driving school wanted me to come in for an interview. I grinned. Freedom was imminent.

•

By early fall I had two adjunct positions for the community college, both temporary and part-time teaching jobs. I quit the misery of the cubicle job and never, ever looked back. I picked up an adjunct position at UNO (this made three!), teaching technical writing and "Writing for Criminal Justice." I was a good teacher, loved it, and so I embraced it. I applied to the PhD program in English at UNL, the University of Nebraska-Lincoln.

And I was . . .

Rejected.

I was crushed. I was used to being praised and applauded, not rejected. I kept adjuncting, running my ass off from one college and class to another, changing clothes and changing identities in university bathrooms, from trucking instructor to writing instructor. It was exhausting. My status as a temporary instructor meant no office and no benefits, and I was driving back and forth twenty-five miles each way to and from Blair, where I had moved when I'd gotten married in 2010. When I wasn't adjuncting, I ran a very, very small vegetable business off what I raised on the seven acres

I lived on. I kept working. I applied to UNL again. I got rejected again. It hurt even more the second time. I kept working.

The following April, I got another one of those phone calls, you know, those calls that set your life on a different course. My cell phone rang on a Thursday while I was in the middle of teaching my criminal justice students; embarrassed that I had forgotten to turn it off, I silenced the phone and kept teaching, soon forgetting all about it. A full three days later—yes, three *entire* days—I noticed I had a voicemail. It had come days earlier when I was in class, and I had overlooked it entirely.

The phone thought it recognized the number and displayed: *Maybe: Elizabeth Egger.* My heart dropped, and then leaped, then plummeted. Elizabeth *Egger.* The UNL English graduate chair. The contact person for admissions. *That* Elizabeth Egger. That Elizabeth Egger called and left me a message that I didn't see for *three whole days*: someone who had committed to UNL was no longer coming, and would I still be interested in joining their program? It's hyperbole to say that I almost died from excitement, but, you know, I almost died of excitement. I returned the call immediately and left a message. Elizabeth called just a few hours later. She was gracious and pleasant and excited to offer me a position in the English program. Of course, I accepted.

Waiting anxiously for August, I kept working.

•

When I began the program at UNL, I was interested in work, but I didn't realize it. Instead I had expressed an interest in women's and gender studies, trying to understand how women fit into roles that were traditionally deemed "men's work." But as I progressed through my studies, it became clear labor wasn't a focus in the classroom. On the rare occasion it was discussed, it felt subordinate to other major categories of identity. And I could see these effects. They were molding a new generation. For instance, when my own students read Daisy Hernandez's *A Cup of Water Under My Bed*, they were quick to condemn her father as distant and quick-tempered and leave it at that, without seeing the ways in which a limited ability to work (and thus, survive), might make his life complicated.

How long has this intersection of academia and labor been a part of my life? When did I begin to care so much about work? How was my behavior and outlook during my undergraduate program shaped by my parents' experiences? I'm still not sure. But what I do know, without a doubt, is that a rupture occurred during my PhD program.

It happened during that first year commuting to Lincoln from Blair, five days a week. I was assigned to teach on Mondays, Wednesdays, and Fridays, and my own classes were on Tuesdays and Thursdays. The Blair to Lincoln commute took an hour and a half from my front door to the door of Andrews Hall, which housed the English department. I had little choice about living in Blair; my husband had a son from a prior marriage whose mother also lived in that small town, so we weren't going anywhere.

Then, one day, everything cracked open. I left the husband, the stepson, the small town, my horse, donkeys, and chickens to start my own life, in Lincoln. Feel abrupt to you? It was.

I had to leave, for my *self* was at stake. Instead of arriving at home at 10:30 at night from an exhausting day and a long commute to someone who asked how my classes were, I would hear insinuations and suspicions surrounding the male friend and colleague I carpooled with once a week. Instead of coming together on plans for the future, my husband grew more insulated and attached to the acreage while I saw the world as an increasingly big place to explore. He wanted to live his entire life on that acreage, which sounded like a death sentence for my own happiness.

I had changed.

Moving to Lincoln meant I had to rethink the ways I supported myself financially. From here forward, it was just me and two huskies. At the time I ended my marriage, I had a multitude of jobs: adjunct instructor, part-time mail carrier, and truck driver hauling cattle feed to feedlots and dairies (again). One by one, I shed those commitments as I moved to Lincoln and found a trucking job that was flexible with my school schedule.

Two years into graduate school, I became a concrete mixer truck driver.

# Feedback

"Jesus Linda," my brother says as he shakes his head and turns his eyes to the floor. He looks back up at me. "You know what kind of people drive concrete trucks?"

"Do *you*? How would you know?" I challenge him, the guy working on a master's in nutrition and whose brutal day jobs for the last twenty years have always been in landscaping. What would he know about it?

"Yeah," he punches back. "We get concrete sometimes for jobs at work. You don't want to hang around those people." His tone paints an image of a crude, dirty driver—no manners, no brains.

Not long after, my ex-husband calls me up for something. I sit on the step of my back patio with the phone to my ear, my new independence glorious. "Are you working?" he asks. "Have you found a job?

"Yeah," I say. After all, I'm taking care of myself, figuring shit out. "I got a job driving a concrete truck here in Lincoln."

There is a slight pause after the news smacks him across a cheek I know is flushed. "Jesus," he mutters. "Those construction guys are really going to love *that*."

# Rules and Regs

I was in the market for flexibility.

I found the job at Midnight Concrete Company online, through one of those websites where you can post your resume and sort through job ads and more job ads. I was growing a little desperate, and very much tired of sifting through postings for jobs that clearly required a large commitment of time from yours truly, time that I'd be able to give in the summers, but that I couldn't commit from August to May during the school semesters. My university required me to teach two classes each semester, and I was still taking courses. I had to be present. But I also needed money.

Graduate school did pay me, a little. I mean, a little. *A little.* I was privileged to be accepted with full tuition remission, meaning that over the span of five years, I could take as many classes as I wanted without paying any actual tuition. School was pretty much free. I did have to pay for some fees which equated to about $1,200 a semester, and my health insurance costs were approximately $400 a semester. Compared to insurance outside this state job, this was dirt cheap. There I was also fortunate.

The university paid each grad student a stipend so they could teach, complete their grad work, and pay living expenses. Stipends for students vary from department to department and school to school, and what I received from my department each year was $17,000.

If considered a full-time job, this would equate to a yearly salary less than my state's pathetic minimum wage ($9.00 at the time). My department contract labeled this as a part-time job though, claiming that the work I would do as a teacher amounted to 19.5 hours of work per week. With my studies, the contract read, this was quite a load.

I was on my own, paying the rent on a tiny house with a fenced yard so I could keep Alice and Agatha, Siberian husky wonder-duo, my best and only friends. We needed to eat, pay the utilities, buy fuel for my pickup, pay health, vehicle, and renters' insurance, and, you know, live. I needed to save money so that when I left graduate school, I had a penny to my name.

I might possibly have made it on $17,000 a year (although my rent was $900 a month), but only if there were no contingencies, ever. Cross your fingers that my truck didn't break down. Hope it didn't need new tires. Pray I didn't get sick. Pray the dogs didn't. My laptop could not break. There would be no buying any extra books. No buying anything extra anything. I could not save.

If I wanted to consider additional work outside of teaching, though, the contract in my hand demanded I must talk it over with the department first.

I needed a job I could keep year-round and I would not, could not, allow anyone to make this decision for me.

I talked it over with no one.

What was I going to do? Talking with someone wasn't going to change my financial needs and goals, and it certainly wasn't going to increase my stipend. Involving anyone else would just be creating trouble for myself.

The scenario sucked, and I thought, worst case, if I was found out I would get a stern lecture and have to quit my job. As long as I could keep up my studies and fulfill my teaching commitments, I'd be fine. I didn't know anyone taking on the kind of job I planned to apply for, but then again, this was the sort of thing you generally kept to yourself. At least I did.

The online application for Midnight had a section where you could enter the hours you were available to work. It looked promising, like an invitation. I clacked away on my keyboard and typed in my schedule. Midnight Concrete was the best shot I had. I crossed my t's and dotted my i's and clicked submit. The rest, as the cliché goes, is history.

•

The building where the driver manager officed was a strangely shaped hexagon just off a bumpy, poorly maintained road, a minefield of jagged potholes eating away at the asphalt. Harold's office felt dated, brown-paneled and nondescript, and it put me at ease. Harold fit his office exactly, a slow talker with a creaking voice that you had to pay close attention to or you'd miss the joke.

I've been on the defensive in every driving interview I've ever had: tense and prickly, waiting for the jab across the face, for the dismissal, for the joke, the look up and down, the appraisal, the question and the doubt.

My brother tells me I say thank you too much, too often. I think I'm polite, but I wondered, was it simply how I was raised? Or how I had been conditioned? "Thank you for letting me do this," I'd later say to the shop manager at my plant for permitting me to work in the garage on a rainy day, lugging a gigantic impact wrench around, changing tires on a mixer truck. "Thank you for having faith in me to do this." He looked at me like I was crazy.

"I can't believe they trust me to do this, that I get to do this," I've thought, grateful and thankful when a friend's husband and his father hired me to drive truck during corn and bean harvest, when I was transitioning from that cubicle to teaching.

Thank you, thank you, thank you, it was a chorus I sang every day, a part of me I still sing.

Does it have anything to do with the automotive instructor who failed me in his classes when I was twenty, ignoring me in lab while he carefully instructed the male students on automotive electrical systems?

Does it have anything to do with my trucking partner at Werner, the guy who drove that day-cab during the twelve hours I didn't, who looked me up and down in a way so invasive that the slimy memory of it still hasn't faded?

Or maybe it was the service writer at the Chevy dealership in Blair, where I spent thousands on repairs to my Dodge pickup, someone I knew, someone I willingly brought my business to, who, when I commented that the good news about an expensive repair was that my clutch bearing had lasted as long as it did, replied "especially with a woman driving it." And laughed.

Or the farmer who had asked me, when I rang him up to ask about the driving job I saw in the paper, if I was calling for my husband.

And on, and on.

So it developed, gratitude and defense, wrapped together in a weird messy ball deep inside my chest.

I sat there on the other side of Harold's desk, dumbfounded, watching him flip through my driving application and say, "You've obviously got loads of experience, we don't even need to give you a test drive." He was right, and I couldn't believe my luck. My experience was complimented, not questioned. Harold quickly had hold of my respect and loyalty.

I was hired. Did I have any questions?

"What do I wear to work?" I had no idea what a concrete mixer driver wore or where a person acquired whatever it was. Harold leaned back in his chair and stretched both arms towards the edge of his desk.

"Construction casual." There was such a thing? As I listened I realized that was Harold's code for saying there really wasn't much of a dress policy at all.

"This isn't a fashion show," he continued. I looked down at what I was wearing. Nice western style jeans, clean square-toed cowboy boots, a button-down shirt. Long hair down and neatly combed. No jewelry. Eyeliner as the only makeup. The outfit no longer fit my personal style, but it was my best professional outfit for an interview as a truck driver. I looked back up at him. I wondered if he said that to everyone.

"So like, tee shirts and jeans?"

"Yes, no profanity, things like that, no holes in your clothes, but you'll get dirty."

Not a fashion show.

•

"You're a worker," Luis says to me over by the wash pit. Apparently they've all been watching. "You'll do alright here, 'cause you do the work."

"We just heard we were getting a woman and that she was teacher," Mateen told me later, after we became friends. "That's it." I imagine who they must've imagined.

"You're a good driver," I hear from Tacks, one of the plant guys, and I wonder how he knows.

"She drives great, does a great job," my trainer Matt says to people we are standing near, more willing to compliment me indirectly.

Years later, the plant manager will tell me he's still never seen anyone finish training so quickly, within a week. All those years later, the astonishment hasn't left his voice.

I take my place alongside the drivers at the Laforte Street plant and get no flak, no hassle, no attitude. Their wings outstretch and I am gently folded in.

•

Throughout the first weeks and months of work, I watch my coworkers and learn what to wear. I go to the farm supply store and find a shelf stacked with $5 T-shirts in "safety orange" and "safety green," (but it looks like yellow!), colors known as "high-visibility" or simply "hi-vis." Working on city streets where people texting and driving is the norm, and on construction sites with dangerous equipment moving on all sides, drivers want every chance to be seen. Being seen keeps us alive. I ditch the bulky western jeans for the skinny variety, whose stretchiness is a benefit as I climb and squat and kneel and sit all day long, my body becoming accustomed to the motions of the work. I quickly wear out the pair of steel-toed boots I had from my last job and buy a new pair, waterproof and with the novel bonus of soles that lessen your chance of electrical shock. Who knew there was such a thing?

In my third summer, the company will decide to give everyone five nice, very breathable hi-vis shirts, a synthetic blend in safety yellow (or is it green?) with reflective striping and the Midnight company logo on the back. They ask our sizes but do not consider that clothes are made differently for differently sexed bodies. Why would they? Men make these decisions. When I declare I need a small, the boss asks, "Are you sure?" When they arrive, my small-sized men's shirts are nice but boxy; they are much too wide for my skinny ass and remind me of a potato sack, but I can roll with it. What I can't abide is that the short sleeves, which look completely normal on everyone else, reach my elbows and therefore look ridiculous, making me look like a little girl dressing up in dad's clothes.

I stand in my bedroom in front of the full-length mirror, twisting and staring, moving my arms, tugging the shirt away from my body to gauge how many of me could fit in it. I sigh.

Rather than fight this particular gender battle by explaining my different body and my desire to feel like a professional adult to the men who made this uniform decision, I take the five shirts to the tailor. To make them work, she essentially has to create a cap sleeve, almost making the shirts sleeveless. My free shirts have now cost me $100. The upside is that I don't feel like a child; I actually feel kind of tough, and the *severe* farmer's tan I get will at least be farther up my arm (and therefore easier to hide in my other life). Yet now the sleeve hole is so big that you can plainly see my armpits and the side of my bra whenever I move. But three years in, I no longer am self-conscious or care if I am breaking a rule. If anyone challenges me, I will just demand they find me some equivalent women's shirts. I buy sports bras in neon colors to complement my new look. It's not a fashion show, but to be myself, there is little recourse other than to be seen.

•

As a truck driver, I perform work that not many women do. As a truck driver in the construction industry, layering one world which excludes women over yet another, I look around and see myself as even more a rarity. This is not a man's world, though it most certainly a world which is overwhelmingly inhabited by men. I am not a woman doing a man's work: I am a truck driver, working. If people would just allow it to be so.

I often have the troubling desire to forget about my gender, but I can't, because both men and women take care to remind me of it as I move through my work. But every day, in a small way, or in several small ways, or sometimes in some huge way, I am othered because of my gender in the space I choose to occupy. Though it feels natural to be where I am, I am a problem. How much of a problem depends on how I deploy my femininity or how I mask it, how I hold my breath and carefully balance myself while walking that razor edge. I am more a problem or less of one depending on whose gaze falls upon me and on how he feels that particular day. I am more a problem or less of one depending on how much I speak my true self. This balance between problem and blessing is like what we term a "straight back" in driving school, backing a semi-truck down a straight line, like you might do down an alley: a series of constant tiny adjustments.

I am not just another truck driver, I am *the woman* truck driver, or as I am called most often, "the girl" or "the lady driver." In my truck, on a jobsite, at the concrete plant, I feel every move I make: hyperaware, I analyze it, because I know it's being analyzed. Little wonder I have an unhealthy level of self-consciousness.

# Sharing

It is 7:45 on a Monday morning and I am leaving the plant with my first load of concrete for the day. It is a late start for a warm May morning, but it rained the day before, and it's muddy everywhere. Mud slows contractors down and makes some jobsites unworkable for a 70,000-pound dinosaur-like mixer truck with a tendency to sink in soft ground. The sky is overcast; my mood is a little overcast. I pull out of the plant parking lot, turning right. I cross the railroad tracks and make a quick left, heading to Meadowlark Boulevard. A small gold car rolls to a stop at the intersection as I make the left turn; I see it on my left in my peripheral vision, I am aware of it as a professional driver should always be. But as I steer my concrete mixer through the turn, an extra movement from the little gold car catches my eye and I turn my head to look at the driver. She is a Black woman a little older than me, smiling brilliantly. Her shoulder-length hair is neat like the patterned button-down suit jacket she wears, its colors the colors of jewels. I can see the glint of her earrings. But most of all I can see that she is staring at me, following my movement in my mixer truck as we turn that corner, my truck and I. Poised at the stop sign ready to turn right, she pauses, moving her head to follow my trajectory. The dazzle of her smile is directed at me. I know this because she catches my eye and lifts her hand up to her rolled-down window, giving me a thumbs up and a nod, still smiling.

    I smile back; there is no time to wave; I am already passing by. As I grin, I feel my own cloudy mood recede, even if it's just for a few moments. What was she feeling as she saw me in my truck? Solidarity? Admiration? As our gazes met, did she have that same moment of connection, that feeling of power, a fleeting moment of encouragement and pride? Her in her little gold car, maybe on the way to her job. Me in my giant white mixer truck, on the way to mine.

## My Pretty Eyes

It's June and I am pouring concrete at an out-of-the-way site for a company called Rocks 'N' Grout. It is owned by Rob Merrell, a white man in his sixties: average height, white hair, a belly, the usual. Always wears white Hawaiian shirts that look like they come from Tommy Bahama. The guy looks like he'd be perfectly at home in a Florida retirement community, while still running a tight ship that leaves both his guys and me wishing he'd be around a little less. Rob is a micromanager, picking at the details of every job even though he's got a very capable team. Anibal oversees the crew, and it is Anibal and his guys who do the good work. Rob drives around in machinery, moving stuff, grading dirt, playing, telling Anibal to do this or that, telling us to pour faster. It is because of this pressure to hurry that I prefer not to see Rob on a jobsite. He's not mean, but I don't like that pressure: it pushes too hard against doing our jobs safely, which is more important than saving a minute or two. Other than this, Rob has never bothered me, never really talked to me, in fact, which is perfectly fine. Just the way I want it.

My fellow drivers consider Rob "a good guy." You know, a cool guy. Someone everyone likes and admires. The man. He's loaded, my guys say, their eyes and voices flickering, quick and back, to another reality. At Christmastime Rob sends a box of Rocks 'N' Grout sweatshirts to each Midnight plant, or an oversized box of chocolate-covered pretzels. So he's generous. Word is that most of these buildings we pour for Rob are also owned by him. My coworkers ooh and ahh over how many square feet Rob's new building is, over how much stuff you can put in there. I don't know the details because the details of owning so much stuff don't interest me. The awe of my coworkers seems silly. Nothing against Rob, but from what I can see, he's just another rich white man using his money to play.

The pour on this June day is a slow one, only three trucks needed. When Bryan, who's in the first truck, finishes unloading, I back in. The lot is really huge, acres upon acres, with more than enough room to turn around in any way you might choose, but because the dirt is soft, Rob wants us to back in in a particular way, so we don't get the trucks stuck. Fair enough. I perform this task with ease, coaxing the transmission into low reverse gear and making a simple, sweeping backward arc around pickups and pallets, ending my imaginary rainbow in just the spot I need to be in, in front of the large dump bucket hanging from the telehandler Anibal has waiting.

I climb down from the cab, pulling on my work gloves as I walk to the back of my truck. Rob stands there hands on hips, and he speaks to me, smiling: "That's about as good a job as I could ever do!"

A driving compliment! "Thanks!" I say. I feel proud for a moment. I straighten my back and my legs, chin up. Then the questions in my head start flying and fast. Is Rob a good driver? What if he's a bad driver and he knows it, so it's sort of a dig? That's ridiculous, why would he insult himself? Why would he go out of the way to insult me? Especially when it was a good back? No, it definitely has to be a driving compliment. Unless it—

My thoughts are interrupted as Rob, still there, utters one more line: "And I like this too," he says, gesturing towards his eyes. "Looks nice."

I look at him, confused, wondering why he would be talking about my face. Then I get it. Rob is talking about my eyeliner, which is black and heavy and drawn out from the corners of my lids towards the tips of my brows. I am so used to wearing it each day, seeing myself in the mirror with it on, that I forget it's not a natural part of me. I nod and thank Rob again, smile, and climb up on the back of my truck to begin the pour. I push aside the surprise that an old man has complimented my make-up. Anibal is waiting.

The pour is uneventful, me trying only to have patience with it because I want to make a phone call. My friend Jaime called just before I backed up here, just as Bryan was finishing his load, so I ignored my ringing phone. It's habit to tell Jaime all the details about my day, and so later I tell him about my driving compliment, feeling quite proud. "I just hope it *is* a driving compliment," I say to him. Because the unfortunate part about being a woman and a truck driver is that you never know.

A week later I am back at that same jobsite, again pouring into the large dump bucket, but one of only two trucks this time. Anibal is there with his guys, and Rob is there too, who, aside from the driving compliment and the eye makeup thing and a few instructions about pouring faster or which way to drive in, has, let me remind you, never spoken to me in my three summers of doing this job. Like, ever.

Again I walk to the back of my truck, pulling on my gloves like the last time. Unlike last time though, I am already wearing dark tinted safety glasses: I have some weird eye infection this week, and it is better for my vanity that no one really sees it. The only thing worse than feeling shitty and gross is having people stare and ask questions about it. As I get ready to pour, Rob is there by the truck, oddly, and he speaks to me again. "With those glasses on I can't see those pretty eyes!"

An invisible wall smacks me, and I hesitate, breath caught, but after that almost imperceptible movement, like a trained monkey or Pavlov's dog, I raise my safety glasses and smile, before quickly lowering them again.

I don't know what to say to you, reader.

Rob leaves, apparently satisfied, and I climb onto the truck again, Anibal and I working in sync, chatting a little, everything fine, except the scene that just passed plays over and over in my mind as I stand there. Why did I do that? Don't I have a mind of my own? I run through a myriad of alternatives that I should have taken, angry with myself. It's a small thing indicative of a lifetime of training. Trained to please, trained to smile. Conditioned to react before I have time to think. I might as well have curtsied.

Old, rich, white, and now unsettling, Rob is driving around in his skid loader, grading the dirt around the wall forms Anibal and his men pour as I stand alone on my truck fender, waiting for Anibal to return again and again with the dump bucket so I can fill it. I chastise myself but let it go little by little, musing over my surroundings and whatever else is in my brain, gazing through my safety glasses at the nearby interstate, semis swooshing by along with morning traffic; at the obscenely large storage building next door that we poured the last summer; at the dirt; at Anibal's men working. It is still early morning but already sweltering, and I want to finish this job, get inside my truck and cool off, have some coffee.

The skid loader approaches with Rob inside, next to where I stand. Without getting out, Rob unhooks one front attachment from the machine and hooks up to another; I see it without really noticing the details. The skid loader spins round in the soft dirt and faces me. Rob pops the front door open and looks at me; he is also wearing sunglasses.

He points up, gesturing. I am confused. Does he want me to add more water to the load? Go faster? I look around and try to figure out if I've missed something in my semi-daydream-state. I begin to get frantic. What does he want? Are we done? Or should I just spin the drum while I wait for Anibal?

Since I am clearly not getting the message, he raises his sunglasses and points to his eyes. "One more time?" Rob says.

Is he joking?

I stare at him.

He can't be serious.

I shake my head no.
"Oh, come on," he says, exactly like a child would. Whining. Like a little boy.

Or maybe, exactly like the old, rich, white man that he is.

"No, please," I say. No *please*? But it does the job. Like a child pouting or a man embarrassed, not expecting to be challenged, he quickly gives up, puts his glasses back on, grabs the door of the skid loader pulling it shut, and drives away. The dust settles.

Anibal and I finish pouring, I clean my truck up, and I leave, fuming and silent and incredulous.

The more I drive, the more I stew, the more I want to explode, overwhelmed with the stupidity of the episode. I have to let it out. When I arrive back at the plant, I look for my buddy Mateen.

I don't find Mateen until well after noon. Actually, he finds me. I am at the plant sitting in my truck, waiting behind several others for a load, when I hear a truck pull up next to me. I see it out of the corner of my eye but don't bother to look up from my book. Then I feel someone staring at me. I look over, and there's Mateen, grinning at me goofily, on purpose so I would laugh. He'd been at the DMV all morning renewing his license; that's why I couldn't find him earlier. I throw the book on the dash and scramble out of my truck and over to his driver's door.

"I missed you! Where have you been?" I ask, climbing up on the steps of his cab after he opens his door to me. It's the usual tale of the DMV, the lines, the waiting. I wait semipatiently through all of this before getting to my news: "You're not going to believe what happened at Rocks 'N' Grout this morning."

When I get to the part about the compliment on my eyeliner, Mateen raises his eyebrows, an open-mouthed, expectant smile on his face as he listens attentively. When I get to the part about the "I can't see those pretty eyes" he throws his head back and laughs so loud and so heartily that it catches me completely by surprise. But after a second I figure, well, he recognizes what a stupid, desperate sounding thing that is for a man like Rob to say. A man like Rob.

When I get to the part about Rob's return in the skid loader, and his request for me to take my glasses off, Mateen's laugh disappears and he lets out a slow and incredulous sounding "Whhhhaat," pulling his neck and shoulders back as if the news will grab him too, and I say, "I know, *right?*" I am bouncing on the truck steps with energy, with disbelief. "Can you even believe that? He's never even talked to me before. And this out of the blue, like a *child.*"

"But, I mean, Rob's always been so respectful." I can see Mateen processing. "We never have any problems with that guy." He looks off into the space ahead of him.

I knock him on the leg with my hand to bring his focus back to my gaze. "But you *believe* me right?" I know he does. He is my friend.

"Well yeah, I'm just really surprised, that doesn't seem like Rob." What?

That was a "Yes, I believe you Linda, of course I do," wasn't it?

"I don't know." I say, hanging off his truck cab and looking off into the distance. "I just wanted somebody to know."

We move on.

•

Other than Mateen, I mention the Rocks 'N' Grout incident to no one. What would I say? That Rob Merrell, beloved and respected by all, wanted me to take my safety glasses off to check out my eyes? It would sound ridiculous to anyone I told it to. Since when had anyone ever been sexually harassed about their *eyes?* Plus, Rob Merrell was *established,* solid. He was a cool guy. The structure that surrounded me at Midnight was male, every brick of that safehouse was a dude: the drivers, the plant supervisor, any other management that I occasionally crossed paths with. There was a human resources department across the street in the corporate office, but "across the street" was another world for most of us drivers. We didn't interact with them, they didn't interact with us. I did not know how to convey why Rob's comment bothered me so much, nor what I would have liked to have done about it. What I really wanted was to record the incident, to have a witness, to be heard, so I did this by talking to my friend. At least Mateen would be able to say I'd told him about something in the past. . . . As stupid as it is, as infuriating as it is, I figured documentation was the best I could do.

Which of course sounds utterly, completely ridiculous. Documentation. It sounds so . . . Human Resources. It sounds ineffective and submissive. It sounds like I have learned the language of corporations, when what I really want to do is just be loud and fucking mad. Focus the anger at its source and have it *do* something, change something.

Because years later I am still so fucking mad. So I analyze it.

What exactly was it that had happened? Why, after years at work had things suddenly changed? Why did Rob suddenly find me approachable? It was not that I had never been approached by men before at jobs: it happened on and off. The Latino men who showed interest were generally straightforward about things, following a pattern of questions designed to dig progressively deeper: tienes una familia, niños, are you married, do you have a boyfriend, can I have tu teléfono? I would shake my head no and guard my phone number like an inheritance. The white guys were laughably chaotic and slow in their advances: obvious too, though they would rarely ask me personal questions designed to discover whether I was single, and never asked for my number. I would laugh and look away and stay aloof until they gave up.

But in these cases, there was not the large power differential that existed between Rob Merrell and me, because of age, owner status, money. I shared a workspace with these other men: we did the same work so, in many ways, were on an even playing field.

Their approaches were for the most part harmless; I either said no or gave off a disinterested vibe and that was the end of things. If anything, I was the one with the power in those situations: because I was an employee of Midnight and they were employees of whatever concrete business, it would be entirely normal (I mean, no, but yes, you know what I mean) for one owner to say to another, "My employee is being harassed by your employee." Since many of the companies we worked with were small businesses that had no HR, no formal employee training, no company lawyer, I arguably had a much larger force behind me had I ever needed to draw from it. My gender caused "problems" and disruptions, and it also made people nervous, was a liability, as I'd come to find out later. And my whiteness and native English shielded me, too, in all its typical ways. So yeah, a level playing field, more or less.

But why now? What was Rob trying to elicit with those comments? I can only think of one answer, the most common answer. Rob was dipping a toe into the waters of attraction, or trying to. I had never paid him any mind except in the capacity of the boss on the jobsite. Were the comments about my makeup intended to change that course, to prod me in the direction of seeing Rob in a different way? What, I wonder, would have happened if I had not refused to take my glasses off? What would have been his next move?

I wonder if it was coincidence that it started with recognition of my good driving. I've always thought that was just Rob's opening line, an observation made into a tool used to situate himself (unsuccessfully) as a desirable sexual object. Fifty years ago, film theorist Laura Mulvey wrote about women's function in film during the golden age of Hollywood movies: that women were in movies to be seen, gazed upon, a spectacle. They were there to be desired, wanted, but there was a problem: those sexy ladies interrupted the scene, got in the way of men getting shit done, of doing what men do.

That was it, that was me: an alien presence, invasive. Backing my way around shit like a champ, not getting bogged down or stuck, standing on my truck fender on higher ground, in control, handling things with great skill and ease.

A threat.

What do you do with a threat?

Make it a part of the story. Make it into something you can conquer. Make it sexual. Be the hero, save the girl. Get the girl.

I fought back in my own way. In the years that followed, I refused the free sweatshirts. Anytime I saw Rob on a Rocks 'N' Grout job, I put on my sunglasses. Smugly. Obviously. Even when we occasionally poured inside a building and the dark glasses combined with the muted light made it hard to see, I persisted. On the infrequent occasions Rob would take over the handling of the chutes, unsatisfied with how quickly Anibal was pouring, I made every effort not to see him: to look out the opposite mirror from my position in the cab, to follow Anibal's directions instead of Rob's. I made him work to get my attention, and then it was a listless, passive attention, not switching my gaze from one mirror to the other until I heard a shrill repeated whistle or saw the others pointing to their boss, and even then I offered only a delayed response, if any at all, to his signals demanding I speed up the drum and pour faster.

Passive aggressive, yes, but it was within my control. Childlike? Maybe it was. You get what you give. I smiled at the others but did an abrupt about-face for Rob, looking off in the distance if I met his pickup while driving out of the jobsite, all of this my subtle middle finger directed only at him. What would be his recourse if it annoyed him too much? A complaint to Midnight, a demand not to have me back on his jobsite? One could only hope! The thought was almost an incentive.

•

It is my body that sets me aside from the other mixer drivers, from the other construction workers.

At Midnight I become hyper-aware of how I stand, especially in the beginning. I want to do a good job. Really, I want to do an excellent job, a perfect job. I stand at the rear of my truck, feet close together, back straight, the controls for the drum held in both hands, near my chest, fingers poised over the start button. Are they ready yet? Ready now? Time to bring the concrete up? What do I do? When the guys ask me to add water, or get the ticket, I scurry off and do it, feeling very much like I am indeed scurrying, feeling very much like scurrying is a female thing.

At other times, like when I am sitting in the breakroom surrounded by the other drivers, I notice the very un-female like behavior of how I am sitting. Slightly slouched. Legs apart. Stretched. Elbows on the table, or arms flopped onto it, like a guy, I guess. Or like myself.

•

It is my body that sets me apart from the other graduate students.

In the classroom, things are quite different than on the jobsite. Here there is no neon sign hanging over my head, buzzing and blaring my difference. Here, it is the smaller details.

With luck, I've remembered to check my fingernails before leaving the house. They accumulate an astonishing amount of dirt, even when I'm not driving the truck. The dust, dirt, concrete, and mud that come with working outside permeate all parts of my life. Back in my adjuncting days, when I commented to a roomful of students that I lived on an acreage and grew pumpkins, the student who sat closest to me immediately piped up with "Is that why your fingernails are always dirty?" They notice the details.

When classes begin in August, I can't throw on a sleeveless blouse or even a short-sleeved one without exposing a startling difference in skin colors thanks to the tan I've received over the summer. The back of my neck, my face, my upper arms, and my forearms are browner than they've ever been. My very upper arms and collarbone and chest are white—white like vanilla bean ice cream. Fellow grad students comment that oh I'm so *tan*. I think and sometimes say that yes, it's because I go *outside*. Most white grad students and professors seem like particularly pale specimens of humans, haunting the hallways of the English department with necks bent and eyes pegged to the floor, which makes the contrast especially striking.

Even though I am familiar with classroom spaces and comfortable in the front of the room, I lurch around like I've just been plucked from my natural habitat. I am always accidently kicking things, my boot or shoe thwacking away at the metal grate along the wall while a student is speaking, or while I am speaking. I make noise. The students giggle. I am too big for the room.

•

From the rear fender of my concrete mixer, I watch the bodies of men. There are, simply and without exaggeration, men everywhere. The men I see are almost exclusively white or Latino, and mostly Latino, mostly from Mexico, Guatemala, and El Salvador. They are of all ages, men in their twenties and thirties, men in middle age, and some older men who deserve to be in retirement instead of looping concrete and dripping sweat in the Nebraska humidity.

I have seen several near identical "Hecho en Mexico" tattoos, but I have seen more tattoos in general here than anywhere else outside a tattoo shop. Sometimes the young Latino men don't look like they are dressed for work; tight jeans slung low, tight T-shirts, hats worn high. But mostly they are dressed for work, for sweat, so much sweat. Sometimes I see chubby white boys or skinny white boys who are clearly some owner's kid, their seriousness about the work belied by the fact they are wearing shorts, wildly inappropriate for a construction job. They struggle to keep up. It is mostly the white men who tend to go without shirts on the hot summer days, their skin a blistering red. It is mostly the Latino men who know better, wearing long sleeves to cover their arms, ballcaps or sombreros, bandanas covering their necks when the sun burns too intensely.

I watch these bodies, how they move and how they are shaped. The muscles in their forearms, their paunchy little bellies, the absence of little bellies, their waists. I see their careful haircuts or their sweaty ballcap hair, their grooming, or lack of it, that speaks to not spending their days working around women. Or maybe it speaks to the intensity of the work they do. Sometimes I see butt cracks and I look away fast, but then peek back, repelled and fascinated at the same time, wondering how they can't feel the draft. I listen to the lilt of voices or the gruffness of those voices, hear them sing, hear them swear, hear them laugh and giggle, hear some call me ma'am and others call me bonita. I make a face when they spit or do that gross snuffling thing with their noses. I watch them bend and straighten, watch them walk, and will come to know many of them from a distance purely by the way they move, just as I will come to know my fellow drivers. From this distance, I feel a growing intimacy with men's bodies.

• 

And then there was Sofía. I couldn't stop staring at her.

In my first summer at Midnight, I don't yet know S&T concrete, who they were or how to identify them. I only have the address of the job, more new construction in Lincoln's "Waterford Estates." The neighborhood is exactly what it sounds like: a new neighborhood on the outskirts of town that was given a name with aspirations, for suburbanites with aspirations of a particular type. Most new construction in Lincoln comes, automatically it seems, with a three-car garage. In some cases, the square footage of the garage is bigger than that of the house. Waterford Estates is a little more ambitious than some of its near lookalikes in this town, like Wandering Creek or Firethorn: it is organized around a manmade lake, the "water" in Waterford. The streets have admittedly appealing names like "Moonlight Drive," "Half Moon Bay," and "Deep Water Bay." The houses are like most houses in the suburban US: brown, beige, gray, beige again. The people living in the houses in Waterford Estates come in even fewer colors.

When I moved to Lincoln, Waterford Estates was a neighborhood in the making (it is still expanding east). Some streets were complete in that there was little to no new construction happening on them, most of the empty lots filled in with new two-story homes, freshly sodded lawns, driveways crisp and free from accumulated oil stains, porches and front doors carefully curated with wicker chairs, an outdoor cushion in a bright color, and pick-and-paint wooden signs in predictable shapes: a pineapple, a flip-flop, the University of Nebraska "N." Other streets were clearly still in development, like 104th Street, which had more homes-in-progress than finished homes with families already moved in, importing their 2.5 children, three cars, golf cart, and a boat for good measure. On streets like 104th, one could witness how new construction happened in stages. Some homes were still just dreams, dirt lots waiting to be sold. Others existed only as basements, waiting for the house to be framed. Framed houses might have windows and siding, or they might not, they might have shingles and gutters, or they might not, they might have sod rolled out or still be waiting for it, a driveway and sidewalk poured, or not quite. A neighborhood like this, a neighborhood up and coming, pops with unneighborly-like sounds: the warning backup beeps of telehandlers and skid loaders, the synchronous tapping of hammers on roofs, the buzz of circular saws, the throaty growl of large trucks, the quiet of concentration on craft, the shouts of jokes made in Spanish and in English to pass the time.

    I find the address of the S&T job, or more accurately, I find the general area where the address should be and see a guy who is clearly waiting for concrete. A good-looking guy with a ballcap and a goatee, he's standing in the dirt at the intersection of 102nd Street and Starlight Bay, a lot on the corner, a house that was still just foundation and basement. He looks expectantly in my direction, and I look back at him. Several other men sit on a low foundation wall, waiting to get started. A radio bleeds musica de banda, pulsing its way through the July heat. The day is sultry and dripping. Watching the goateed man hold his hand in the air, rotating his wrist with index finger pointed toward the sky, I know he wants me to turn around and back into the lot. And so I do, turning my truck south and lumbering over the curb of this corner lot in low low gear, crawling across the dirt. The man, who I have since come to know as Enrique, the owner of S&T, backs me up to the skeleton of this house to what will become the garage. The street, the foundation bricks, the other boxes that make up this subdivision, they are all the same gray color.

The other men sit, waiting while the boss and I sort things out. Where does he want to start? How many chutes will we need? He kids me a little. Shy and still finding my footing in this new world of construction-banter, I fumble my way through a friendly retort. Then chutes on and truck ready, I climb in the cab and we pour the garage floor of this future-house. Nearly finished, I wait for the group to see whether they have enough concrete on the ground, or if I need to pour a little more. And that's when I notice that something seems off. Something's odd here.

I am out of the truck, standing at the back. When I have a moment to watch, the group of guys in this crew stop being a group. One by one, I study each of them. All are Latino. Two are a little older, two a little younger. One of the younger ones . . . I can't believe it. Am I really seeing this? One of these guys is a beautiful young woman.

She wears a white long-sleeved tee with the S&T Construction logo on the back, tucked neatly into her jeans. Her black hair is barely visible, tied up under a white bandana, under a large-brimmed straw hat with a small, high crown, string tied under her chin. As she gets closer, I notice a gold ring in one nostril, a small tattoo behind her ear. A few black curls escape from under the bandana. Rubber boots, typical of a concrete worker. Young, maybe twenty-five?

She doesn't look at me as I watch. I feel like a creep. I stare, rudely, I'm sure. I try not to. She speaks with the others in Spanish, all of us moving slowly in the heat, everything seeming slow in the heat. The concrete is very wet, and it slops around their ankles in small rough waves as they all wade through it. As two of the men screed the concrete from the back corner of the garage, the woman and one dude give a few synchronous pushes of their loops, a rake-like tool used to move concrete. Then they stand back and wait for the others to progress. The woman is anything but still; she turns and moves and rotates and sings. She never looks at me.

I can't believe my eyes. I can barely look away. Another woman, out here?

I'm ashamed of my staring. Even in this moment, I understand that this is what men must feel when they see me arrive on a jobsite. She is so unexpected that the shock of seeing her holds me captive. Knowing this does not help relieve me of my fascination or my creepy gaze.

When we are done pouring, it's time for me to wash my chutes and clean up my truck before returning to the plant for another load. I pull the truck away from the garage and park maybe twenty feet away, still on the dirt lot. I scrub away in the heat, still distracted. I glance up every now and then at the men, and her, finishing the concrete. I notice her begin, I think, to walk by. She stops and approaches, shouting a little: "Where did you get your tattoo?"

I look over and smile. "Omaha."

"Can I see it?"

I pull back my left sleeve, already rolled back to lessen the extent of my farmer's tan, and point here and there: "This is San Francisco, this is London, and this is Colombia . . . they're all places I've traveled." She stands on the other side of my chutes and cranes to look at my arm as I turn it from side to side. But my mind is too far ahead to focus on tattoo conversation, already on to things I am dying to ask.

"It's really nice to see you here." It is the best I can articulate, still in shock over seeing another woman in this space where I expect to see only men.

She pauses for just a moment, looking a little startled, before her face melts into understanding. "Do you ever see any other girls when you are out here?"

"No," I shake my head in emphasis.

"No, me neither, but the other day we drove by a place and I saw two, and I was like looook!!" She points into the air in front of her and mimes her own self, staring out the window of the imaginary pickup.

"I know, that's why I was so excited to see you!" I babble. "I always think I'm just out here doing my job, you know, I'm just me, and I don't understand why people think it's so different. But now that I see you, I get what they must feel like. It's weird, because I don't feel special . . ." I am definitely babbling, excited. She nods in agreement, but I don't know if she understands. I am not explaining myself well. "How long have you been doing this?"

She squints and thinks. "Thhhrree years."

"Wow! Do you like it?"

"I do!"

"Why?" I am killing this conversation.

"I like to feel the sun . . ." She leans back, lifts her chin to the sky, and her arms stretch out to hug the sun that is bearing down on us all. "And moving around!"

"Yes!" I pause. I want to keep going, but I feel pressured (by nobody) to keep working. "What's your name?"

"Sofía."

"Sofía. I'm Linda. It's really nice to meet you." I have gloves on. So does she. There are the chutes between us. We don't shake hands.

"You too." She smiles and starts to move away. I bend back down and resume scrubbing the drying concrete, looking up and then away at Sofía.

•

Maybe I'm a unicorn. Maybe Sofía is too. That's my private joke sometimes, that I am like a unicorn in this construction world, something that's not supposed to exist. Rare, something that turns heads, that you'd have to see to believe. Trust me please, I'm not egotistical. It's just that, well—

I sit at stop lights in my truck and feel like I'm being watched. I look down and to my left and see that I am actually being watched. Maybe it's an older couple in the car next to me, her in the passenger seat pointing up, clearly saying, "Look, look at the lady truck driver!" to the man by her side. It might also be a car full of men, a single woman, anyone really, but they are there from time to time, staring, gesturing, pointing at the strange zoo exhibit they see in the lane next to them. A mixer truck is already a billboard, and there I am, pasted on it. I am on display. I am the girl on the billboard in the song of the same name that Dennis taught me so many years ago.

"And I'm like, 'Quit looking at me,'" young Katelyn says one day, another driver who works at the Prairie Park plant. We rarely see each other, but when we do we talk and discover we have the same experiences. We talk and it feels so strange, to find someone who knows exactly what I mean because the same things happen to her. Katelyn finds it awkward to be stared at when she's driving, and I get that, but I've grown accustomed to it by now.

It happened during training when I first learned to drive a semi; my female trainer and I pulling a full-length van trailer out of a Petro truck stop, me driving slowly, cautiously through the intersection. We both watched a small SUV pause to let us pass and saw the woman behind the wheel mouth something to her younger companion as she points. Although we couldn't hear her, it's obvious what she's saying: "Mother and daughter," she wrongly assumed.

It happened during my first real trucking job, when I hauled that cattle feed in a 49-foot walking-floor trailer. If the farm was new to me, I'd park the truck on the county road and get out and walk the place, looking for the bunker where I needed to put the feed, checking for obstacles before backing the trailer in. I'd come upon the farmer who could see me but not the truck, and despite my uniform, the same khaki shirt that every driver wore, the cognitive dissonance was too much. "Can I help you?" he'd say, startled to see a strange woman appear. I'd explain that I was looking for where to put the feed, and he'd stare blankly then surge into action, finally putting the puzzle pieces together.

In Nebraska and Kansas, farmers and their families usually live at the feedlot, the houses only a stone's throw from where trucks unload and cattle are fed. I made regular deliveries to a place in Columbus, Nebraska, thinking nothing of what I was doing, just backing in the trailer, operating a few buttons and levers to open the trailer door, move the floor, unload thirty-one tons of feed. Then I'd button it all back up and drive away, onsite no more than thirty minutes. The first time I met Joe, a salesman for the product I hauled, he laughed and told me, "You know, Bill's daughter-in-law was having a baby shower when you delivered to his place the other day. It was there in the house. One of the women saw you and then they were all over at the window, watching you through the blinds." And I had no idea that whole time. I pictured a bunch of baby-drunk ladies, piled on top of one another, trying to get a glimpse. I hoped I wasn't pulling my underwear out of my butt. I was fascinated by their fascination with me.

It happened when I taught truck driving school, and these were perhaps the best times, because then it was me in a semi-truck leading a band of young men, and there were always light jokes at the truck stop we frequented about who was teaching who. My students, mostly twenty, twenty-two years old, proudly corrected the hecklers, and I loved them for it. Nick and Doug were two of my favorites, a little older, calm and wise and witty. As Nick drove one afternoon through midtown Omaha, Doug sat in the backseat of our Kenworth and watched Nick perform, watched traffic go by. I sat in the front passenger seat, giving Nick tips and helping him shift if he needed it. "Hey Linda, don't look now," Doug piped up, "but that whole car of guys next to us is staring at us." I turned my head to the right and looked down. The car full of men stared straight ahead and I grinned.

"Did they all just whip their heads back around?" I called to Doug. He laughed. Of course they did.

But despite all of that, the unicorn analogy doesn't hold. I'd love to believe in unicorns—I've been enchanted with them since I was a girl—but unicorns don't *really* exist. Katelyn and I do. Josephine and Debbie and Rena, other mixer drivers I would meet over my Midnight Concrete years, they exist too. Sofía exists. The handful of other women I see working concrete, maybe five out of a thousand, they are real. We are here, boots on the ground, wading through concrete or feathering a clutch, breathing, sweating, solid, strong, so strong.

Was my reaction to Sofía any different than when men encountered me on the jobsite? The unicorn who strutted in one day, out of nowhere?

It was, because it was a desire to be seen by her. I felt a thrill when Sofía asked me if I had seen other women "out here," because it meant that our difference was also something *she* thought about, which meant that I was not, actually, alone. I wanted to dive deep into her experiences, thoughts, and feelings, and I wanted her to want the same thing from me. I wanted to have more than just a moment of recognition; I wanted solidarity, female friendship. Of course I wasn't thinking any of this at the time, although as I drove away, I fantasized about what I should have done, if I had stopped again and asked Sofía for her number, asked if she wanted to have coffee with me sometime, asked if she wanted to talk.

As I write this now, I am surprised by the pull the moment of recognizing Sofía still has over me. I go through my days loving my male coworkers, my quirky brothers, feeding off fulfilling, compassionate friendships. Although there are times I feel ostracized or alone due to a situation, or a customer, or a cultural norm I am not a part of, I never feel totally by myself, because I can always go to a friend like Mateen and have someone to listen, someone to comfort me, someone who will do his best to understand. Until I experienced moments like I would with Sofía, and later Katelyn and a few other women, I never suspected that perhaps I was lacking something. Never having known female comrades in work, I didn't know what I was missing.

# Truth and Beauty

He is my best work friend.

When I started working here, I couldn't imagine we'd be friends. Not one single hope of it ever happening. Mateen seemed like the cool guy, so why would he bother with me?

But four years in he leans through my cab window, dodging my fist bump and grabbing my hand instead, squeezing and shaking it: "Hey, you know I got your back no matter what happens," and I say, "Oh I have no doubt," and nothing has ever been truer, but I am laughing too and also wondering is something about to go down?

Two summers ago he came to my house on a Sunday to help me dig my garden. I know what's going on with his kids, that his wife has a part-time job serving lunches; that when he was young and working at a factory in Charlotte, he dated a woman named Verlida, and oh were they ever something, and that was after he had to leave someone else a world away. He knows about my school, my challenges with teaching, my struggles with loneliness, my dating ups and downs. He says if I want to meet someone I should go to bars, or I should try online dating. When I ask if he'd try online dating, he looks at me askance and says, "No, I'm married." When I ask would he try online dating if he wasn't married, he throws his hands up and smiles and says, "If I wasn't married, I'd go back to my country!" We don't agree on everything.

I come back from my first vacation, and he surprises me by putting his arms out in an embrace, saying, "I'm glad you're back." The years slip away and when he turns fifty, I bring donuts, the good expensive ones from the all-night donut shop, and he puts his right arm around my shoulders and tells a coworker, "My friend remembered my birthday," and I beam.

Our conversations dance around different cultural values. Sometimes he surprises me with how forthcoming he is, at other times with how conservative he seems. He tells me in year one that he can feel the racism every day, and I feel then like he might know how it is with me and sexism. In year four I urge him to speak out with me against management and he yells, "They are white, Black, American," waving an arm in the general direction of all of us, and I fight back tears. I can't fix everything. Our trucks are parked next to each other at night, assigned spaces in the line side by side. We wave at each other when we meet on the road, make faces and jokes in the passing moments when we are all scrambling for loads. He is the first one I look for when something happens, when there is something I want to talk about.

Mateen says in his singsong voice, "You want some more cookies?" and dumps palmfuls of crackers into my hands. Mateen is a fierce constant softness as he flicks his cigarette to the ground and gently adjusts the buckle on my coveralls before I can finish asking for help. I see how focused he is on the task and know that my friend loves me too.

# Participation

"This is the construction industry," on repeat, "This is the construction industry, and it's not for everyone." You know better, you know this for what it is; it is both clever rhetoric to weed out rabble-rousers and something they truly believe. They are so invested in this single masculine way that to dissent about a work practice is suddenly not to fit. This is not for you.

You know better, but still, it digs in. Sometimes you want to leave, but the thought is terrifying not only to leave the driving that you love but to feel somehow as if they would be proven right. That you couldn't hack it in the construction industry.

And on the other side, you sit tucked into the conference table in the graduate seminar room and feel like you are watching a ping pong match, head bobbing from left to right as you witness the verbal sparring between other graduate students, many of whom are in their twenties, so much younger than you. The dread accumulating in your stomach because a big chunk of your grade is participation but how are you supposed to participate when you can't even get a word in? It's worse than that, because you honestly don't know what to add to the conversation, your brain working on some other wavelength or on some different sense of time. An idea will come to you later; now, you have none. You sit and sink deeper under the sister senses of shame, embarrassment, and stress. You know better, know that you couldn't have come this far if you were an idiot, but knowing that doesn't help one bit when it comes to generating a thoughtful contribution. When you finally see how something relates to trucking and manage to speak, there are light-hearted laughs and a few eye rolls. The heavy feel of the room haunts you like they might be proven right.

# And Yet Another Instance Where a Word Wields Its Power

I walk back to my truck through the parking lot and stop short. I stare at Arthur in his cab. What—what is that he's doing? Head bent down and glasses on the tip of his nose, Art's staring intently at the steering wheel. I sidle to the side to view this weird behavior from another angle. That's when I see a book propped up on the wheel.

That, I think, can't be right.

I climb up the two steps of Art's cab and hang onto the truck mirror, sticking my head up near his open window. "What-cha got there?" I ask, but by now I can see it. A book of wordsearch puzzles.

I get caught in my nearsightedness. Except for Matt and his crossword puzzles, and Stevie and his western novels, there are no readers or puzzlers here. Art especially catches a lot of flak from the other employees, teased because he marches to his own drum. To see him with a printed puzzle in hand is totally unexpected.

What Art tells me next amazes me: he tells me part of his story, about which I have never bothered to ask. The word search, a tangible artifact of words, opened a door I should have opened long before. He sits in his truck seat, and I hang off the door, chin on my arms listening. Art tells me that he had loads of trouble learning to read when young, so his dad brought home a word search book. "It didn't help me with phonics, although the dictionary did," he explains, poking the word search pages with his index finger. "But this, it helped me recognize words." Art is a sixty-one-year-old Black man with eight children, and he gifted every one of them with a dictionary when they turned five or six years old. Words are that powerful to Art.

I hang there and listen, and Art talks then about his grandchildren who are teachers, pausing now and again, tilting his head to think of the right word: "But as a teacher, you're *rich*." I smile. He explains, continues to teach me. "As a teacher, generation after generation after generation, you teach one and you teach another one and another one and it just continues to live on."

I stare. I have never heard him talk so much, and I am transfixed by Art's memories of words, their impact on him, and their impact on his family. "I *love* words," he says. "Words are powerful. Words matter. You have to be careful how you put them together, because they can hurt people."

Like words, in Art's eyes, teachers have power. I can see, watching him speak to me, unguarded and easy and smiling, that Art has done what he could over a lifetime to put that power in the mouths of his children. His advice to his youngest son, whenever he would have trouble in class, was to speak up. "There's always a choice," Art says. "You have to say:

"Excuse me, I need help.

"Excuse me, I don't understand.

"Excuse me, *no*."

Then his speech slows and softens: "Excuse me, I think it's time for me to go."

•

# And Yet Another Instance Where a Word Wields Its Power

My curiosity piques when I hear people talk about the power of teachers, especially if they don't know I am one. Arthur, of course, knows this about me; he's seen me walk through the Midnight lot on countless mornings, dutifully hurrying to class. When I heard him describe the intangible riches one reaps from teaching, I felt a swell of pride. He isn't wrong. Many of the moments when I have felt richest have been when I am teaching for free. For years I have volunteered to teach adults in various capacities, whether it was as a one-on-one English language tutor or the instructor for a class in citizenship, English learning, or GED education. To be a small part of their experiences compares to nothing else.

As I prepared for an English language class not long ago, I sit at my tiny kitchen table by the window, head bent and multicolored paper scattered everywhere, hell bent on making flashcards to help my Spanish and Arabic speaking students learn the English verb "to be." I write pronouns on orange paper, verbs on green paper, articles on blue, nouns on hot pink. With a satisfying screech of the fat marker, I write plural and singular nouns. Ecuadorean. Soccer player. Dog. Marker. Machine operator. Grandfather. Mail carrier. I write words that relate to my students' lives.

I pause over mail carrier, realizing I have almost written mailman. I look at the word, black marker hovering in the air. I think about how each of my students will learn that they have a mail carrier, not a mailman, and how easy it would be to teach them another word, any word. The choice is entirely mine. The way they will be introduced to much of the English language is under my control. To gender or not to gender. Of course, I stick with mail carrier.

I wonder how often teachers think about the many ways they can so casually wield their power.

•

I am nervous. I am about to embark on a journey through a graduate seminar in nineteenth-century Latin American literature. I study literature, yes. But I study it in English, and this is the first class I've ever taken where Spanish is the language of instruction, aside from courses designed to teach Spanish. Teaching the language is not the point here; in graduate Spanish courses, students are expected to know Spanish. As I'll soon learn, many of the other graduate students are native speakers: from Mexico, Spain, the Canary Islands, the Dominican Republic, Colombia. My reasons for being here are twofold and overlapping: a pull to learn about the world outside the United States, outside of what I've always been taught in school, and because I want to improve my Spanish. The world is big, and I want to talk with more people in it. I can't improve by staying in my comfort zone. This class is a risk.

Is my Spanish fluent? Yes, but there's so much I don't understand. I make a ton of mistakes. High school, my only prior stint with formal language instruction, was over twenty years ago. The rest of my learning has been a self-directed puzzle. Rosetta Stone. Reading the short stuff by Gabriel García Márquez, ever so slowly. An excellent workbook in grammar practice. Some short travel experiences in Spain and Colombia. Speaking at work with whomever is gracious enough to do so with me. Thanks to the travel, to the people who've informally taught me, thanks to work, thanks to Jaime, my Spanish is peninsular, Colombian, Mexican, Guatemalan. It is a beautiful mixture of almuerzo, and sometimes lonche; of mulera, troquera, or camionera, depending on whom I'm talking to; without vosotros or vos, but full of chejes and tecolotes. I use nosotras in mixed company, Thanksgiving becomes "chumpipe day," and I chao chao everyone I meet. I notice that sometimes, even my English constructions are inflected with Spanish influence, and I wonder if this is partly why my dissertation adviser keeps rearranging the word order in my sentences.

On the first day of this class the professor blows into the room with a firm "Buenas tardes," and after a moment of readying the instructor station, rolls directly into explaining the syllabus. If the behavior weren't enough, the tidy maroon dress shirt, slacks, and neat silver hair tip me off to how class will be conducted, to the mood. I look around and am startled to see only two other seats filled. This is good, I think, they won't kick me out for my slow Spanish. They need me for enrollment.

The instructor speaks fast, or it *seems* as if he does. It just sounds fast to me, coming from a different language background. Yet I know the context so I can follow along well. Prior to class I dissected the syllabus and translated the words I was unfamiliar with. I feel ready. I sit in my desk, excited and dutiful, listening to this man explain the course policies and the homework. Then, with no interruption or pause—had I not been expecting it, I would have missed it, the professor's sentences rolling towards me in continuous waves—we arrive at the moment for class introductions.

There were always introductions. In preparing for this first class, I had thought carefully about what I wanted to say. I needed to think about it beforehand so I could get the words right, refine it. The night before, I had asked Jaime, who had been my most consistent teacher up to that point, talking every day with me for the last six months, "Asi es 'Soy estudiante postgrado y soy camionera, o soy una estudiante y una camionera?" Did I need the article or not? He corrected me, we ironed things out. I was ready.

The first student says her name, Lucia, that she is from Madrid, and that she is here for a year. Or maybe that she *had* been here for a year. That's it. Introductions are going to be short and sweet. The second student, Chuck, states his name and that he is from Lincoln. By looking and listening to him, I had assumed that he wasn't a native Spanish speaker (which turned out to be correct, although his fluency seemed effortless). And that's all the information I get about Chuck. Is that really *it*? Why aren't they saying more? We are chattier in the English department.

It's my turn. I remember Jaime's words, his advice to me; I *had* been remembering it, in fact, this entire time, breathing the words in and out like a meditation exercise: "Don't be nervous, if you are nervous, you will forget." I'm not nervous, I can do this, I'm not nervous. I suck in my breath, puff out my chest, and say proudly, "Soy Linda, soy una estudiante postgrado en el Departamento de Inglés, y. . . ." I look around.

According to the model, this is where I should stop. But I want to keep going. "Estoy muy nerviosa." Why did I say that? Mentally I slap myself on the forehead. "Soy camionera." The magic words, which almost always work, work here just as they do in the English department. I'm a truck driver. This yields a reaction from the room. I am unstoppable now. "Manejo un camión de concreto para Midnight Concrete Company."

The professor grips the podium and leans back. He seems delighted. "Muy bien, muy bien, una camionera," he says, holding on to his podium and nodding. Is his hard exterior softening a bit? He pauses and looks toward the back of the room, into space, then at me, and says in English, "I get my concrete from Beatrice Concrete."

All I needed was an opening. The dynamics of the classroom urge me to be silent, the unfamiliar language gnaws at me a little, but I want to know. I ask him, in Spanish and with some rookie errors, what he does with the concrete. His own projects, he says. He asks me if it is hard to drive such a big truck, or maybe it is more of a statement, but I take it as a chance to speak. More or less, I say:

. . . that "en el pasado, manejaba un camión mas grande, así esto es mas fácil, pero bien porque hay muchas cosas distintas a aprender"

. . . and that "por ejemplo, con concreto siempre estamos lavando el camión, hay mucha agua, y es un poco difícil en el invierno, sabe . . ."

. . . and in response to a comment about hard work or skills, I say, "y a veces tengo la oportunidad a ayudar mi amigo en concreto, poniendo el concreto y finishando, y es mucho trabajo pero es muy interesante, aprendiendo nuevas cosas . . ."

I keep glancing at the others, at him. "Lo siento, puedo hablar de esto todo el día. . . ."
"No, no, esta bien," the professor says. "Me da la oportunidad de escuchar tu español. Tu español es muy bien."
"Gracias," I blush. It *is* muy bien, for a mostly self-taught gringa who's still learning every day.
He looks into space again for a moment, chuckling a little.
I wait.
He speaks. He plucks one single word from my speech. "Finishando. I love it, that's really great." He chuckles again, not meanly—he doesn't say this meanly, just introspectively—but I reply, "Oh, lo siento, mi amigo es de Guatemala . . ." looking around the room. I had picked up on what he was getting at. Finishando wasn't a real Spanish word.
El profesor wraps things up quickly from there; it was just time to move on. But it is a long time before my focus returns to the

matters of the class. Finishando. When I said my friend was from Guatemala, my intention was to explain that we used different words for things. Like finishando. Just different words for things. When we were working with the concrete, we were finishando. I can't profess to know with certainty why this crisp, sharp professor was laughing. I can reason that it was because of the supposed barbarism, the messiness of the word finishando.

I sit there in my little desk, trying to follow the lecture that is rapidly unfolding in front of me about Latin America's independence from Spain. I feel heavy and hot with shame. I hear the professor speaking, but it's as if the time is flowing right past me, rippling by me, and I'm a stone, stuck in a moment. Mi amigo es de Guatemala. A treacherous sentence, in this context. I know why I said it. I was grasping in the language, not taking enough time to think before I spoke. I wanted to explain that Jaime drew from a different word bank, his own variety of Spanish. I felt instead that I had implied something entirely different. Implied his words were different, subordinate, less than, because of where he was from, because of what he did for a living. What damage had I done with that line? Finishando. Mi amigo es de Guatemala.

If I could go back, and I want to go back, I would not say lo siento. I would say, pues, "Mi amigo es de Guatemala, y es mi maestro en muchas cosas. Somos trabajadores, y decimos 'finishando.'"

•

Here's a fact, profesor: finishando is a Spanish word. "Finishar" or "to finish" is, in linguistic terms, a préstamo, or a borrowing from one language to another. It is a word created to fit the context and the environment, to fit a need.

One could say something other than "finishando," although it would be like marbles in the mouth. One could say, for example,

"Estoy acabando con el concreto": I am *finishing with the concrete*, meaning in this context that I am finishing up the job, I am almost done. It is not quite the same thing as saying finishando. Perhaps then, one could say, "Estoy dando el acabado": I am *putting the finish on* the concrete, or in other words, making it smooth and without flaws. This is closer, but it is a mouthful.

What fits the communication need the best is this: finishando. Perfectly. Legitimately.

•

Writer Gloria Anzaldúa might have many names for the word I'd learned from Jaime: part of a border tongue, a forked tongue, an anglicism, a patois, a mixing of English and Spanish. Finishando is a borrowing from a contact language. It's logical and flexible. Imagine creating words to fit a need, to fill an empty space. The dexterity it takes to mold and bend, to find a solution, to innovate. I see this on jobsites and at Midnight all the time, the wordplay, the jokes, the ways to make things more efficient.

My enrollment in that Spanish class necessitated that I read and write a lot in Spanish, things I'd never done much of before. I was now in the academy in Spanish, and I was at work in Spanish, and I was in the personal in Spanish as long as Jaime and my ELL students were in my life. I was happily surrounded.

Yet the immersion in a classroom setting was jarring.

I wasn't ready for how my use of finishando revealed me, how it revealed to others where I came from and with whom I spent my time. In English, I could code switch when I wanted to, but in Spanish, I didn't know enough to realize what I was giving away, to know what words or constructions would be red flags to others. There was no way to put on a mask. It was not the first time I had been judged by my language, but it was the first time like this. It was the first time with so many strings attached, sitting in a classroom, an environment I had lived in all my life, an environment I was comfortable with. Being called out about finishando felt like a signal, another fucking signal, that I did not belong.

I knew that the native Spanish speakers I shared this classroom with likely faced this struggle outside of this department. And all of us, because we were wrapped safely in the arms of academia, where they corrected us, but still taught and embraced us, had still more protection than so many of the people I worked with.

•

I am in the fourth year of my graduate program. It is time to take my comprehensive exams. I should actually have taken them the year before, but I'm behind. You might imagine why. A full-time driving job and a part-time teaching job and homework . . . something was going to give, and of course it had to be my schoolwork. I could keep up the responsibilities to others, had to, wasn't going to let anyone down. So my stuff came last. But with a big push from the graduate chair, I finally made my reading lists, had them approved, and decided to take two timed exams rather than create a portfolio of writing that I'd be judged on. Exams seemed like a better fit for me, even after I learned most people choose to do the portfolio. To sit still, be brilliant, and write for three hours, twice, under the pressure of a clock, may not be appealing, but it was the best choice for me.

In my master's program we were *required* to take a timed exam based on reading lists. I aced it, garnering a "high pass." The letter that informed me of my grade read, "This grade is evidence of your exceptional ability to work independently, to synthesize diverse materials, and to write with clarity, focus, and effect." One of the professors who evaluated my exam told me later that I had said things he and the other reader "had just never heard before." That felt incredible. I had every reason to be confident about my ability to do it all over again.

For my master's exam, I had explicit guidance to focus on writing and the content quality of my answers, told not to worry about spelling or other proofreading concerns. The professors—who would determine if I passed or not—would focus on the substance, on what we could say in the three hours allotted for the test.

I find no such guidance when my PhD comps come around at UNL, maybe because so few people choose to do them. Other than the time limit, there are no written rules.

When the day comes, I'm nervous but I feel prepared, until the exam questions arrive in my email inbox. They are nothing like what I had expected, and worse, perhaps because of my nerves, I have a hard time discerning what it is I am being asked to do. After fifteen minutes whip by, I can barely even see the screen, the stress blurring my vision. The directions about how many examples to give for each part of a complicated and layered question are confusing, and I spend too many precious minutes trying to figure this out. When I take the second exam a few days later, things keep going downhill. This exam was compiled by two *different* professors who formatted their requests completely different from the two professors days before. Again, I waste time trying to interpret what it is I am supposed to do.

So I write. And write and write. I am a writer who proofreads and corrects as I go, rather than revising after a work is complete. But I am writing in a frenzy: sweating, thirsty, continually twisting around to stare at the clock which has such a heavy hand in determining my fate. I write, not worrying much about my spelling or grammar, I just write.

Several weeks later I receive the results. I passed. Each of the four professors has written her own response to my answers. They are all positive and supportive, though the final part of a response by one of the professors catches me off guard. She is surprised by the approach I took to answering the questions: more exploratory than conventional, she says, my writing informal, a risk, though it was a successful one.

I am surprised, indignant, defensive. I was writing about working-class women's writing and activism, texts that often deal in spaces outside the university. They are about working women whose speech and writing take a variety of forms. And I write the way I think, the way I speak. I am hurt that my speech seems to fall short. The processes I am so concerned with researching, how academia marginalizes working class subjects, are working on me in this very moment.

This is my language register, the space I've carved out for myself inside my native tongue. This is what I have to offer. Sure, I know how to perform academic language, but it's far less natural to me, and because it seems so obviously performative, I opt out whenever I can. I know too that my everyday speech has changed because of where I spend most of my time: at work. I've picked up expressions, words, and syntax from the guys I'm always around, from what I hear. My natural mode of expression is a thoughtful, meandering hypothesis inflected with a vocabulary accessible to the people I care most about. I know these comments come from a professor who wants me to succeed, who is here to help me, but I feel like I've just barely skated by.

I wonder still: why was it important for me to write formally for this exam? To demonstrate that I can do so, I suspect. To demonstrate that I realize the gravity of a formal exam setting, perhaps. I just wasn't following the script.

But when I was taking the exams, it didn't occur to me that there was a script I was supposed to follow. I didn't stray intentionally. Despite years of graduate school, surrounded by online catalogues, resources, journals, erudite peers and professors and all of it, there were these moments when I discovered that I didn't know something I was *supposed* to know, that I *obviously* should have known given my immersion in this place. Thinking, perhaps, that I could be me and still be successful here, thinking that I would fit—perhaps that was the risk.

Looking back, though, perhaps I knew what I was doing the whole time. I realize the difference between how I spoke with grad students and how I spoke with construction workers. I knew how much I code-switched, talking a certain way with coworkers when I was angry or fired up, or when I wanted to make a point: academic talk became a tool in my arsenal when I needed backup because it made others uneasy. But just as interesting was the extent to which I brought the speech of construction sites into graduate seminars for the very same reason.

My trucker talk—and I'm not talking about swearing, we are much more nuanced than that stereotype—set me apart. It disarmed competitive situations, nervous moments. It made some people roll their eyes and think I was a dumbass, and it cost me a lot at times, yes, but it also made people smile, made them think I was "so cool." Not performing what was most appropriate was to hide *and* to be seen. In refusing to talk in a way I neither wanted to do nor could do well, I was making space for myself in the often stressful, grinding, pressure cooker environment of the university, and also asserting the presence of the working class in a space that otherwise ignored it.

**Please**

Look out for yourself, and each other.

# Legal Protection

The rumor on Wednesday, spread, as usual, by Ratt, was that we had an early pour this coming Friday, one where we had to be on the job at 4:00 a.m. "On the job" means at the construction site with our trucks loaded and ready to deliver—not, as one might think, "on the job" at our plant site, ready to clock in for work.

On the job at 4:00 a.m.: I could put a few things together and do the simple math.

According to Ratt, the job was near Ceresco, which was enough to tell me I needed to figure thirty minutes' drive-time. Fifteen minutes for loading and quality control testing the first load. Fifteen minutes for the pre-trip inspection of the truck we did every morning upon arrival, and our supervisor always added a fifteen-minute cushion between this and the actual time the first truck would load. That was one hour and fifteen minutes' worth of stuff to do, which meant the first group of drivers would need to arrive at work at 2:45 a.m.

I did my personal math. I tried to leave the house fifteen minutes prior to my start time. I like to have one hour and forty-five minutes to get ready for work in the morning, although I am always tired, so I usually rose with about an hour and twenty-five minutes to shower, eat, take care of the dogs, dry my hair, dress, make my lunch and my coffee, and hug the dogs goodbye. This meant an alarm set for 1:00 a.m.

It meant two alarms set: the "drop dead" time of 1:00 a.m. when I had to get up, and the pre- alarm at 12:45, so I could hit snooze just once and enjoy the bliss of lying there for a few more minutes, squeezing Pingüino and moving my feet back and forth enjoying the softness of the sheets, the darkness of the room, what passed for rest.

I was on high alert Thursday, the day prior to the early pour. After three summers at Midnight I'd been learning a lot. We had only started this early once before, at 2:30 a.m. my first summer, to pave a new parking lot for the school district's buses. And there was a 3:15 a.m. start a few months ago this year. I cannot even remember what we poured.

To understand my heightened sense of concern, you must understand several things. One is the federal laws that surround the hours a driver can legally work and can legally drive. The second is the way Midnight seemed simultaneously both oblivious and highly aware of these laws, depending on the context. And the third is the cult of silence that seems to permeate the driver force when it comes to the enforcement of these hours-rules. We know these rules exist, know we can personally get in trouble for not following them. Trouble with our company yes, but also with the Department of Transportation, or in other words, with the State Patrol, with people who hold the power to affect whether we can work *that day* but also whether we can work *at all* by continuing to hold commercial drivers' licenses. Hours-of-service rules, or the HOS, are in place to protect the motoring public (from drivers falling asleep at the wheel) but also to protect the driver (from abuse and overwork by their employer). And yet, as a driver group, we rarely talk about the HOS or about harnessing the protection that the law can provide.

Our collective silence lets the law protect someone else instead. Let me explain.

The Federal Motor Carrier Safety Administration governs how long truck drivers can legally work in a day and in a week. We are permitted a fourteen-hour workday, and within this time, we can drive a commercial vehicle for no more than eleven hours. The fourteen-hour period starts when we arrive to work, and the minute it ends, we can no longer be behind a wheel. This fourteen-hour period is called "on-duty" time.

Between each on-duty period, the law requires a ten-hour break before you can begin a new day and a new fourteen-hour on-duty period. After reaching seventy hours of on-duty time or an eight-day work week, whichever comes first, the law again requires a break, but this one for no less than thirty-four hours. This is called your "thirty-four-hour reset." It's your weekend. There is one notable exception to the fourteen-hour day, and that's the sixteen-hour exception: you are permitted to extend your on-duty period to sixteen hours for one day each week, as long as you finish your work in the same location you started from.

I find Malachi, the plant foreman and the man responsible for communicating start times to us drivers, working in the back of the building, remodeling what had been a changing room for the plant guys into an office for the new operations manager. That manager, Lenny, is also there, along with Howard, our lone office guy at the Laforte plant. I interrupt their chatter to ask Malachi, who is the middle of mudding drywall, if the early pour is still a go, and if he has a rough idea of when we'll be starting.

Yes, it's still on the job at 4:00 a.m., Ratt's gossip is correct. Lenny and Malachi then engage in a thinking-out-loud arrangement of piecing together start times, with Lenny coming up with 3 a.m. but Malachi with 2:45, just like I did.

"Okay, that's fine," I state, as if I had any sway in making the decision. "I just wanted to know so I can watch my time today and make sure I get ten hours off before. I'm not working until six tonight and I'll call dispatch if I need to . . ."

"Absolutely." Malachi emphasizes the word and nods his head in agreement. Lenny stands there with his hands on his hips and leg awkwardly bent like he does and nods his head along with Malachi. "Actually," says Howard, "it's eight hours off. Ten hours for federal, eight hours for state."

I swivel my head to look at him, a fast response: "That's fine," I say, "but I'm not taking less than ten off. If dispatch doesn't let me off, I'll see you at six tomorrow morning." Now I have my hands on my hips.

There is no pushback on this in the room. We all have different stakes in this game, but Malachi and Lenny and Howard are closer to us drivers than anyone in the dispatch office, both literally and figuratively, since dispatch is located at another plant, in another building. This proximity gives us some degree of sympathy, some understanding. Which is kind of funny, really, because many of the dispatchers have been drivers, while Malachi and Lenny never have (Howard drove more than a decade ago, before the office role).

So where does this delicate solidarity come from? From seeing our faces each day, watching us interact with each other, watching how we work at the plant, seeing the dramas of our relationships as coworkers unfold. On the contrary, dispatch knows us, as we know them, superficially. Our bodies, our faces, our physical expressions are invisible, our personalities conveyed through our voices, what we say or choose not to say on the CB. They know us through the information that comes through their computers: how long each of us takes to perform a certain aspect of the job, where we are at any given moment. They know us, perhaps, through what they hear, or don't hear, from customers when they call in to order, or complain. They know our names, but they refer to us by truck number on the radio, "Midnight to 138" or "Central Dispatch to 242" a common exchange. The ways they know us—the management onsite versus the hidden management of dispatch—are entirely different and yet entirely intimate in the ways that a work relationship is. Because it *is* intimate: we sometimes spend more than half of our day here—certainly the majority of our waking hours.

I turn back to Howard because, I am embarrassed to admit, I hadn't known that there were different hours regulations for *intra*-state trucking. My prior experience was entirely *inter*state. But as I learned in that moment, where federal regulations required a ten-hour break between each on-duty period, the state only mandated eight. Where the federal guidelines required a thirty-four-hour reset, the state required only twenty-four. Unless one of those workdays utilized the sixteen-hour rule, in which case federal regulations overruled state guidelines, and required a thirty-four-hour restart.

In sum, what I had just learned was this: the legal protection I could lean on to support my body's demand for rest was less than I believed it was. Only eight hours legally required between shifts. On the outside, I don't think I flinched. On the inside, I died a little.

To start at 2:45 a.m., theoretically then, you could work until 6:45 p.m. the night before. Get home at 7:00 p.m., make and eat your dinner: now it's 8:00 p.m. You rise at 1:00 a.m. to shower and get ready, so at 8:00 p.m., that's only . . . five hours away. If you want to play with your dogs, watch Netflix, read a few pages of a book, wash the dishes that have built up in your sink, that five hours quickly shrinks. It's a situation not unsimilar to the one writer Barbara Ehrenreich found herself in as she tried to earn a living wage by taking on two minimum wage jobs, leaving her hotel housekeeping job early to make her waitress shift on time: "So much for what Marx termed the 'reproduction of labor power,' meaning the things a worker has to do just so she'll be ready to labor again." There is simply no time.

Can a person sleep for five hours and go to work? Certainly. Can they function? Certainly.

*Should* a person sleep for five hours or less and go to work at 2:45 in the morning, get behind the wheel of a vehicle that will weigh 70,000 pounds when fully loaded, in the dark, and be expected to drive defensively for twelve to fourteen hours, responsible for the lives of others on the road, of the men and women buzzing around the truck on construction sites, for her own self?

Consider your body carefully. Consider what the job entails. Make sure your mental picture shows a sweltering ninety-five-degree day and that you spend a significant part of your working day outside, in the sun, the wind, the humidity. When you are not outside, you are inside the cab of your Mack truck, being bumped and thumped and jostled with every undulation of the road, bombarded by the noise of the engine, the noise of the plant, the noise of the traffic, the noise of the construction site, the noise of the CB radio. And then there's this: the pleasure driving can bring is constantly interrupted by daggers of adrenaline, spikes of unpredictable yet constant stress as the average motorist cuts you off, brakes hard in front of you, runs traffic lights, and performs an array of other stupid stunts that puts their lives and your career in jeopardy. When you are at rest, if you rest, you rest in your truck seat, trying to find room for your legs, trying to find a way to rest your back, your neck, your butt, all of it.

What disturbs me is that, over time, I've normalized working twelve-plus hours a day. I no longer see it as odd. I've internalized it, as have my coworkers. To the contrary, what has become odd is the idea that there are people who work only eight-hour shifts. Fourteen hours, yes, it's a long day, but it's not bizarre. That's my thought process now. Starting these days at 5:00 a.m. is normal, not early. To hear folks talk about *getting out of bed early* at 6:00 a.m. or thereabouts becomes laughable. To consider what it might be like to work an eight-hour day is even more ludicrous, unthinkable really. I have become so used to my reality. Ehrenreich writes in *Nickel and Dimed*, "What you don't necessarily realize when you start selling your time by the hour is that what you're actually selling is your *life*." Imagining what it would be like to only work eight hours a day, the things I could do with my time seem endless.

•

In the history of United States labor reform, the eighteenth and nineteenth centuries saw fights for the fourteen-hour day, then the twelve-hour day, then the ten, then the eight. "Eight hours for work, eight hours for rest, eight hours for recreation," a motto of that early reform, is math even I can do, and it makes sense, doesn't it, when you think about how to divide time not only pleasantly, but to keep the body healthy and sane. A hundred, a hundred-fifty years ago: these times are hard for us to imagine now, so removed we are from those days. Individual workers—people with dreams, fighting for their rights—have been effaced by historical terms or time periods and it becomes easy to forget their flesh and bone and joys and hurts, the things they held closest to their hearts.

In short, even in the nineteenth century, people wanted to do more than work. They wanted to experience the life they were working for.

•

For those of us who labor with our bodies, there is no escaping the marks of that labor. Some of these markers will be visible for a day: dirty fingernails, dust-caked hair, work-worn clothing sweat-stained and rubbed thin at knees, elbows, and wrists. Some of these markers will be visible for a lifetime: callused hands, misshapen fingers or feet, hunched backs, poor eyesight, deafened ears. Other markers will not be so obvious, like the effects of exhaustion, the lack of sleep.

Even a job you kind of like can make you bitter when your new normal becomes a lack of sleep.

It's funny now: When I first thought through this, an occasional 2:45 a.m. start was *early*. But things got exponentially worse the next year: 1:00 a.m., 2:30 a.m., 3:00 a.m. starts all the time, then 4:30 started to seem late. Then a turn back to 1:15 a.m. And you never knew. Sent out via text the afternoon before, these start times would be mixed with 5:30 a.m., or 5:00 a.m., maybe 6:00 a.m. for the newest drivers with the least seniority.

Your weekly schedule was jacked up, as we put it to each other. Jerked around—2:00 a.m. one day, 5:30 the next, 1:15 the day after—how was a body supposed to adapt? How were we supposed to plan?

It can't, and we weren't. "Work," Sarah Jaffe writes, "has no feelings. Capitalism cannot love . . . we might have the best possible boss in the world, one who does genuinely care about us, but they will remain a boss, and financial concerns will come first for them." Finally I got my wish; in this one way, work wasn't about my body. Management did not really care about our well-being, despite lip service about not being able to "make any of this happen without you." That was true, of course, but the sentiment was used as a flimsy façade to mask the true priority. Despite the frequent preaching we heard about being a work "family," when rubber met the road, it was just about hauling concrete. Butts in seats. Drive that truck. Concrete equaled dollars. Drivers didn't matter.

# I Was Talking to Bob and Said:

"You should have seen the shit 138 and I had to do at Tom Potter. It was crazy—"

"You are 138."

"We're two separate entities. So when I pulled up I didn't see a basement, or—"

"What's that?"

"What did you just say?"

"You said, '138 and I.' You are 138."

"No. That's because he's him and I'm me. We're two."

# Assets

When I started working at Midnight Concrete, I knew that mentally, I'd have to learn the ropes, learn about hauling concrete, learn new things. Besides earning pretty good money, that's what made the job exciting.

What I did not expect was the process of learning that *my body* would have to undergo.

Week one and my body was covered in bruises. Each time I looked down, a new one appeared. Astonished, because I didn't know where they were coming from. I couldn't remember running into anything, dropping anything on myself, anything. But the evidence was there, in tender blacks, blues, and yellows. The bruises blend and fade to greenblue and yellow make green, so says the Little Golden book I had as a girl.

Week two was a continuous cycle of bruises and scratches and scrapes coming and going. Minor stuff, I knew. But I had never been able to see forces working on my body like this. As I learned how to operate a concrete mixer, I looked at my body and saw hints of what this job would do to me long term. The week before, my left knee was black and blue in three different places. Climbing up and down the ladder on the back of the truck, hurrying always, accidentally slamming my bony knee into the metal grating and grimacing with the pain.

Three weeks in and my training long over, the mysterious bruises still happened. My right upper arm had three black marks the size of fingertips, just visible below my sleeve. It looked like someone grabbed and squeezed, the grip unrelinquishing. I rotated my arm and there were more. Three more below, and one in the middle; now it looks like the face of a die. My left forearm, just under the elbow: more bruises, bigger, in no particular pattern. I only saw them in the morning as I raised my arms in front of the mirror, standing there to marvel at these new developments my body had produced.

I wondered what caused this. I hypothesized. My body and my truck's body, the big hulking awkward metal body that is my concrete mixer. My body versus my truck's body, running into each other as I get used to his presence, how to move around him, how to work with his moveable parts, how not to run in to his non-movable ones. I am tall, reasonably limber, skinny and bony, but still soft. I am 138 pounds. My truck is tall and inflexible and fat and not soft at all, nowhere is he soft. Colliding with sharp corners of aluminum and steel leaves a mark.

I end up scratched too. Scratches don't stay as long. They barely skim the surface. Their origins are also more certain. In the ninety-plus degree days of summer, concrete hardens so fast, and as I scraped my little brush up and down the sides of the chutes to clean them, I felt the sting of hardened concrete mark my arms. I was surprised later when I saw the marks, then again, I was getting used to it.

Each succession of bruises and scratches will disappear of course, yet do they ever *really* disappear? Four weeks into the job, I returned home at night feeling like my body had been run over by my own concrete mixer. Or that I'd been tossed around in the drum of my truck, in full charge with the idle up. My body was beat, marks or not. I felt beat. I moved slowly when I moved at all. I only wanted to do something that I hated doing: sit still on the couch, go to bed early, night after night. My body demanded it. My dogs demanded a walk; they are Siberian Huskies, after all. We went when I could. I made too many excuses to them. One night I made it off the couch and out the door, but we cut the walk short. My knees felt like they would give out with each step, trying to keep up with two strong Alaska-bound canines leaping toward every squirrel they saw. Often I was in bed by nine o'clock. Nine? I'm only thirty-eight. My body was ruling. Midnight Concrete was ruling. As beat as my body was, my mind felt primed and happy when it could push through the fog of exhaustion. My body could not move but my mind was full of thoughts about the day and the people I met and the things I hoped for. It looked forward to things happening. What will I see today? Who will I talk to? What will I learn? Where will I go? Estaba rendida, so exhausted, but I was happy. Is it only a matter of time before my body adapts and will cease to feel run over? Maybe it has just forgotten how to move. Or maybe it never really learned.

It is impossible to forget that I work outside. The weather is always on my mind in the mornings, thinking about what to wear, thinking about what to bring. In the summers, when you feel like you are on fire or in hell, the decisions are easy and the morning routine is the same. Prepare to sweat. I dress to be as cool as possible, slopping sunscreen all over my face, neck, and forearms, pulling my hair into a braid to keep it from sticking to my neck, trying not to overheat. In winters, it's layers, layers. Long-sleeved tees over long-sleeved tees and sweatshirts, hoods or stocking caps, neck gaiters and long-johns, overalls over long-johns (and jeans to change into if it gets too hot for the overalls). The body rules: if I don't protect it, keep it comfortable, everything else becomes infinitely harder.

•

It is early spring in 2020, and all my coworkers from Laforte Street are gathered in a basement conference room at the nearby Railtown plant. It's a nice conference room, bland but it's warm here, and there are north facing windows at the top of the wall that let in enough light to scatter the soulless feel. But maybe it's warm in here because of so many bodies; the room is barely big enough for the twenty-five of us to crowd around double desks, like those of a classroom, arranged in a large rectangle, open at the front of the room where a projector screen sits.

I am happy to be gathered with all my coworkers at once, the nature of our jobs keeping us at a distance from one another, always together yet always apart. This feels like a reunion, although it's really just a dull annual safety meeting. Also present are several of the management team, who come and go throughout, too busy to spend an entire morning with us: Peter the general manager of Midnight, the truck boss Harold, two members of the safety team we call Betty and Safety Steven, Ian the Department of Transportation guy, and a few others even less familiar to me.

My observations of my coworkers over the years, both at Midnight and at other places I've worked, tell me this: we the drivers and the yard laborers, those of us who do the physical work for anywhere from ten to fourteen hours a day, endure these meetings with mixed feelings. What are we to learn from people we see only a few times a year, always in settings like this, people we rarely see out in the field, who don't ride in trucks, who don't spend any time worth counting at jobsites? From people who come to these meetings and talk at us but not with us, who observe with arms crossed in the back of the room, as if to make a quick escape, to keep from mingling with the common driver. Gloria Steinem writes, "Anybody who is experiencing something is more expert than the experts," and those of us doing the experiencing know this well. There is a limit to what we can we learn from those who have never done what we do, and never will. Guys whisper while presenters are talking, crack jokes. Understandably, the guys half scoff at this event, at our required presence here, but I think there is a shy interest too. Not, I suspect, an interest in the material itself, but a latent desire for involvement, for the chance to be heard.

At the very least, I want to be heard.

I make a few generic responses to questions we are all asked, to introduce ourselves, to share one of the biggest challenges we face as part of our job. Next, I volunteer a frustration, voice shaking (for although I like to speak up, I get nervous), about my incredulity at the company's failure to provide a lunchtime or break for us drivers as part of their standard practice (a monstrously huge problem and exploitative practice to be sure, so stay tuned for the sequel). The other instances are a response to something Betty says.

I have some respect for Betty, because despite her lack of knowledge about our experiences, she appears to have a genuine desire to engage with our voices, if not our minds. I don't remember what table of data Betty had on her PowerPoint, if it is the number of accidents and incidents we had in the past year, or injuries, or number of loads hauled, or something else. It is something like this. But I remember her voice rings crystal clear:

"You guys are our biggest assets."

"But Betty, we are not assets, we are *people*." I do not even bother to raise my hand or request a moment to speak. This bursts out of me.

Everyone looks at me, and at Betty. She is startled. "Okay Linda, but you know what I mean."

"But your words *matter*. The language you use *matters*." I pause. "But maybe that's just the English major in me."

Betty makes some token acknowledgment of what I've said and resumes, though perhaps a little more on her toes, just a little. It takes only a moment before I berate myself silently for qualifying my comment with "the English major in me." A lifetime of implicit training not to speak, to listen, to give the "right" response. In one strong little outburst I showed my power, but then I took my own power away.

The assets at Midnight Concrete Company are the trucks it owns, the equipment listed on the insurance, the replaceable components of metal and rubber. The trucks are assets. The drivers are people.

•

Work marks the body, in ways good and bad. It is tempting to see only one side or the other. Seeing only the harmful effects of hard work cause us to unduly pity workers, a slippery slope toward a classist (and racist, and sexist) perspective. Workers have power too. Literal power in their bodies to perform jobs with skill, efficiency, and dexterity, and cognitive power that solves problems no less complex or important than what white-collar workers wrestle with. Work has made me stronger, in body and in mind, even if I've been banged up along the way. A tendency to romance the laborer and a powerful body, a hard-working temperament, the sacrifice of doing a dirty job: this hurts us. This honeymoon perspective makes it too easy to equate workers with tools.

And that is a great danger of academic programs that include a diverse spectrum of areas of study but fail to include labor or working-class studies: they enable university students—the future safety managers and HR personnel of the world—to ignore work, to see people as tools, if at all. Perhaps this is by design. The university is a place where middle managers are cranked out and schooled to fit neatly into an economic system that serves the interests of those at the top of a capitalist system, oppressors in every sense of the word. School is a place where conformists rise to the top, and those who don't fit the mold don't. So perhaps it comes as little surprise that a place that is seemingly so well poised to study the lives, challenges, and interests of working people is also so well designed to overlook them.

Look—it is not as though the material isn't available to counteract this practice. Academia and books aren't the be-all-end-all; meeting and talking to people have taught me the most in life, *supplemented* by reading. But literature can be an *entry* point for talking about work and the body, and there's plenty of evidence in books documenting the effects work has on bodies, evidence that gathered steam during and after the Industrial Revolution in the late nineteenth century. For instance, in the 1871 novel *The Silent Partner* by Elizabeth Stuart Phelps, the heiress to the town's textile mills, Perley Kelso, is impressed by the mill workers she sees leaving her factories, "Women with peculiar bleached yellow faces . . . [and] bright eyes. They looked like beautiful moving corpses." The obvious contradictions in Kelso's description show us as readers how easily workers can be romanticized: despite sallow skin and a deathlike appearance, these young women still seem beautiful and bright.

And they might well be, but romanticizing any group of people is not only an ignorant move, it is also a strategic one, serving the needs of owners and managers well as they herald the valiant laborer for what she does and willfully ignore the unalterable physical sacrifice that comes at personal cost to her. I have sat in safety meetings and been praised, along with my coworkers, for our skills in handling a giant death-machine safely each day, over and over again, "jumping in those trucks like it's nothing, making it look easy." The praise feels good and does inflate my ego, exactly as it's designed to, and even the most well-intentioned and innocent praise (with no ulterior motive) does the same—it focuses or refocuses a worker's attention on feeling good about what they can do—feeling pride, hyping them up—and diverts attention away from real safety concerns. In *The Silent Partner*, Kelso's comment is contextualized by her counterpart, a young millworker named Sip who identifies the women Kelso spots as cotton weavers, commenting *without* romanticizing: "You can tell a weaver by the skin." Work marks those of us who do it, marks us physically, which can lead to long-term consequences to our health. It also marks us socially, in the immediate, those physical tells combining with others to give away clues to our occupations. It's easy then for all this to come together to enable the world (yes, capitalism again, the greedy, those with money and power) to get one up on us, throwing up walls whenever we try to get around them, too tired to fight.

The detrimental effects of work are present for everyone who is employed, but especially for workers made vulnerable because of fewer choices available to them: workers barred from certain jobs because of their (supposedly lacking) education levels, their English language skills, their immigration status (or perceived status), their race or ethnicity, or the way they display gender or sexuality. Anyone who hasn't experienced this firsthand (like so many of my college classmates) can at least get a taste of this through pages and words. At least since Sinclair Lewis's *The Jungle* (1906), novels have documented this: *The Jungle* is an extended description of the nasty and brutal ways immigrant laborers died from working in early twentieth century-packing houses. In *The Disinherited* (1933), Jack Conroy's protagonist spends his young life moving from job to job after both his father and brother died in the coal mines; asking himself near the end of the novel as he digs ditches for a wage, "which is the more comfortable death . . . being smothered in a ditch or squashed in a coal mine" (Conroy also writes brilliantly about education pitted against work). Literature has always documented what happens to laboring bodies, but it's critical to remember that it's not *just* literature, not just the stuff of books. Lewis wrote what he saw with his own eyes, and Conroy wrote what he lived. Mike Gold, another working-class writer who grew up in early twentieth-century New York, minced no words in his novel *Jews Without Money* (1930): "America is so rich and fat, because it has eaten the tragedy of millions of immigrants." Time has changed nothing: wealth and opportunity are built on the backs of others, others considered assets to the growth of business. During my first four years working in construction in Lincoln, at least two construction workers died on the job—workers Rocael Lopez-Lopez and Mason Harris. It's still a real possibility for many, every day.

And there are the social markers. Ehrenreich writes about the large gap between the ways she was treated depending on whether she was wearing her waitress uniform or her maid's uniform. Within working-class jobs, there's still a hierarchy. While her waitress's polo served as a "conversation starter," the maid's uniform prompted a variety of rude behaviors from others. Ehrenreich explains:

> Then there's the supermarket. I used to stop on my way home from work, but I couldn't take the stares, which are

easily translatable into: What are *you* doing here? And, no wonder she's poor, she's got a beer in her shopping cart! True, I don't look so good by the end of the day and probably smell like eau de toilet and sweat, but it's the brilliant green-and-yellow uniform that gives me away, like prison clothes on a fugitive.

In my cattle-feed-hauling days, I would sometimes stop at the supermarket on the way home from work too, in my work clothes of course, wearing winter overalls crusted with mud and cow poop: I probably smelled, and I definitely looked dirty. I arrived home the first time laden with grocery bags and the question from my now ex-husband: "You went to the store like *that*?"

How else should I have gone? Should I have spent extra time to drive home and change first, as if to erase where I had just come from, what I did for a living? This strikes me now, recollecting, as even more suspect in a town of 8,000 that survives today because of a major corn processing facility and its proximity to local farms. Was it okay to come to town dirty as a farmer, but shameful as a worker who provided a service to those farms? Or was it okay to enter the Family Fare grocery dirty and stinky as a working man, but embarrassing as a woman?

Now, dressed as a construction worker, it's even easier for my work status to be seen when I stroll into a store to do my shopping, covered as I am in hi-vis. I cannot help it, always pressed for time, there is no luxury of changing and pretending. I am comfortable with that. I enjoy doing what I can to be seen, as a physical laborer, to make us workers present and noticeable in spaces where we aren't expected.

If you think I am taking things too far, I ask you to consider your own position as a worker, literally where you sit, where your perspective comes from. For the weavers in *A Silent Partner*, their roles are named: they are "hands" that work in the mills. Phelps writes of this moniker:

> You are so dully used to this classification, 'the hands,' that you were never known to cultivate an objection to it . . . Being surely neither head nor heart, what else remains? . . . Hayle and Kelso [the mill's owners] label you. There you are. The world thinks, aspires, creates, enjoys. There you are. You are the fingers of the world. You take your patient place.

Naming a group of workers for a part of the body attempts to deny them participation in a world outside of that in which the body is used for work. As the workers become their bodies and their bodies only, they become unwillingly consumed by those who have the privilege of not needing to use their own bodies in the same way. They exist only so the rest of the world can enjoy itself.

This is the danger of labels and of language: "hands" may be an unfamiliar or outdated term today, yet the way in which rhetoric functions to keep people in a certain place has certainly not disappeared. This is why I am continually frustrated by the blanket use of "guys" to refer to all of us in Midnight meetings when I am, quite obviously, not one. A small word, yes; a big effect, yes. Thinking about saying something other than "guys" takes effort, but that effort might bring to surface the realization that, as in my case, we are a varied population of workers, with needs that overlap *and differ* because of things like race and gender.

# Conviviality

Juan, Aurelio, and Juan's two sons and I stand in the driveway approach talking about Thanksgiving. Juan's oldest, the one who looks most like him, finishes leveling out the small concrete patch as the other men, older and young, lean on their loops or dangle tools from their hands as I stand there in between.

We stand and laugh and we make the most of two languages, relax for a moment, job almost done, as the homeowner walks down the driveway from her American dream house. She approaches, small and neat, a clean-cut bob and smart glasses, tidy down coat and shiny boots.

"Hi," she says tentatively, looking up, glancing at all of us as we stand there, now quiet. "I just wanted to ask, to make sure if you're doing it right," she begins, pointing at the water main valve in the middle of the patch that Juan's son has gingerly sculpted the new concrete around. "If it doesn't pass the inspection, well I don't want the concrete torn out again. I just want to make sure that's right."

Her eyes go from one of us to the others, and I feel us gazing at her as a group, silenced by her interruption. She looks at me and latches on, and says, "Can you explain to them what I said? I think maybe they don't understand English."

# ¿Pero dónde están los hispanos?

*"They always tell stories we already know."*

So utters Martin Eden, the main character in the 2019 Italian film adaptation of Jack London's novel of the same name. Martin and his wealthy young girlfriend Elena are leaving the cinema; we've seen flashes of the film they watch: a couple kissing, a red rose, a man embracing a woman in a wedding dress. The scene in this film is accompanied by fanciful piano music, and viewers see Elena and Martin arm in arm in the theatre, Elena smiling and engrossed in what's on the screen, Martin's body language betraying his impatience with what he sees.

As they walk out of the theatre Elena remarks that the film was "lovely," and Martin, with pent-up energy, disagrees: "They always tell stories we already know . . . There are billions of stories to tell." When Elena rebukes Martin by describing his own writing as "too raw" and too full of pain and suffering, he gets angry, criticizing her for her nearsighted critique from a very privileged position: "The guy with the full belly doesn't believe in hunger." No matter how well read she is, Elena doesn't, according to Martin, know the half of it. There are billions of stories to tell.

•

I tell this story with the permission of my friend Jaime Echeverría Hichos.

The story of Nibs the missing cat and his rescuer, my friend Jaime, takes place one winter day in December. Jaime and a friend, Edy, both from Guatemala, are preparing a basement for concrete in Prairie Village, one of the many new housing subdivisions within Lincoln. Jaime is a small business owner who specializes in concrete flatwork: driveways, basements, patios, sidewalks, floors. Like most December days in Nebraska, this one is windy and bitingly cold.

Most basements in new homes are completely open when the concrete is poured. Only the foundation walls of the home are constructed at this point, no framing has been done. To get in and out of these big holes in the ground requires jumping and climbing, either a short ladder or some nimble legs. When Jaime and Edy hop down into the basement and begin working that December day, they find a cat sheltered in a small hole between the foundation wall and the earth. The cat is shaking badly from the cold. Jaime's first thought is that the cat must belong to a neighbor, and he is ready to take it from door to door to find out. But the cat wants nothing to do with being picked up and carried around and prefers to hunker down in his hole. That's when Jaime sees a phone number on the cat's collar and calls it, thinking he might reach the owner. Instead he reaches Lincoln Animal Control.

Jaime explains the situation to the animal control officer. The cat is alive, he explains, but very cold, and he is worried about it because the weather is already snowy and windy. The officer asks if the heat is on in the basement, which in recollection made Jaime laugh. "Es sólo un hoyo en la tierra, no es nada!" he tells me. "¿Como a calentar?" He explains things again, gives the officer his name and number when asked, and continues working until an animal control officer arrives about an hour later for the cat, whose name is later revealed to be Nibs. The officer brings a small cage into the basement and takes some photos of the cat. The three men talk for a bit before the officer is on his way, only after Jaime offers to help lift Nibs and the kennel out of the basement.

And as far as Jaime knows, that's the end of things. But later that evening a familiar face pops up on news channel 1011's Facebook page: it's Nibs. To Jaime's surprise, the linked video lays out a very different version of the cat's rescue earlier that morning. He shares the video with his brother, who also works in concrete construction. After Jaime's brother Willy watches the news clip, his first comment to Jaime is a perceptive question: "¿Pero dónde estan los hispános?" Where are the Hispanics? Where, indeed. It takes Willy no time at all to observe and articulate that, one, the people who rescued Nibs were not included in the story and, two, the result was a tidy exclusion of Hispanic or Latinx peoples from the narrative.

The news story itself is titled, "Missing Cat Found in Home's Foundation" and opens with a close-up of Nibs, the black missing cat. The white anchors lead with the following remark: "A Lincoln woman says she has some construction workers and animal control to thank," before the pair hand the story over to white reporter Abbie Peterson. Peterson frames the story with several important lines: "Nibs had been missing for days when animal control contacted his owner, telling her that he had been found in the foundation of a home that was being built." (Note the very effective use of passive voice, how well it disengages Jaime from the story). The next line serves as the transition into the news footage and the story: "Finding his owner was something that was made a lot easier by a simple step that she took." Peterson stresses the word "she," giving extra emphasis to the main actor in the sentence, Nibs's owner. In fact, Nibs's owner has somehow already become the main actor in the whole damn show, despite being on the receiving end of things (no doubt Nibs was, literally at some point, deposited joyfully back into her arms). We might logically expect that Peterson would have said instead, "by a simple step that *construction workers* took, or better still, that *"business owner Jaime Echeverría* took," but this isn't the case. Although we know "some construction workers" are to thank for the rescue, we have just been told, thanks to the way the story was framed, that both the owner and animal control are responsible for Nibs's return. Although "Missing Cat" begins with the claim that the construction workers are responsible for the rescue, that is one of only two times they will be obliquely mentioned: only a few lines in, the narrative already shifts the focus (and hence, the credit) onto others.

The story transitions to footage of Nibs safely restored in his owner's house, which viewers can assume is newly constructed based on what we can see of the carpet, walls, and surrounding room. The owner, a young white woman named Kelsey Yeutter, along with Peterson's voiceover, tells the backstory of the disappearance: Nibs was gone from home for longer than he'd been gone before. The implication was that this was overnight or several nights. Yeutter tells the camera that it was cold: "the wind was blowing, the snow was blowing," and about how nervous she was, nervous enough that she almost didn't go to work. Peterson describes Nibs's current, post-rescue state: he was happy to be home now but a little shaken up, still covered with dirt and mud. We see Nibs being held and stroked, then parading past his scratching post, indeed with bits of mud stuck to his fur.

Next, Peterson is standing outside the foundation of a newly constructed home. It is dark; we can see a dusting of snow over the dirt. Peterson explains that this home is only a few blocks from Yeutter's house, and that Nibs was found "in the foundation." Viewers are shown still photos of Nibs, and Peterson explains that the pictures were taken earlier that day when he was found "by construction workers." We see Nibs tucked away for cover from the weather in a hole between the dirt and a wall, just as Jaime described.

Peterson narrates, "Yeutter says, 'Luckily he wasn't buried in there.'" Just as the description of the weather stresses the danger Nibs was in when he disappeared, so does Yeutter's comment about the danger that *could have been*. It is an especially nearsighted comment if you pause to consider what it means: Yeutter implies (although I think it is subconsciously) that construction crews could have buried Nibs in the basement while working, when in fact, they went out of their way to rescue him. From listening to this narration, it is obvious that for the owner *at least*, Nibs is fortunate to be alive. Finding this cat was a big deal. The voiceover tells us, "Lincoln Animal Control credits the fact that Nibs was licensed, making the process a lot easier for everyone."

The next scene cuts to a white man in an office, wearing a dress shirt and sport coat; the caption tells us he is Steve Beal with Lincoln Animal Control. Beal's first comment appears to respond to the last thing Peterson's voiceover says, the comment about the license. He says, "It's less stress on the animal 'cause they don't have to go into the shelter and wait until the owner either calls us or calls down to the shelter." This is a key part of the text. Notice that the story moves from Peterson commenting on licensing making "the process" easier directly to Beal talking about how "it's" less stress. What process? What "it"?

There is a large omission here. No one talks about how Nibs got into the hands of animal control. Although the reporting claims Yeutter has workers to thank for her pet's safe return, their actions are written out of the narrative. The narrative praises a process and not the people.

The story ends with one final interview with Yeutter. She talks about the process of licensing your pet and how easy and cheap it is, which will make a lost pet a found pet that much more likely. As the story closes and we are about to cut back to the news desk, viewers are presented, once more, with the photo taken of Nibs curled up in the foundation.

It is striking that this story about a missing cat happily returned home in the middle of winter completely omits how that happened, or rather, transforms that rescue into something that was done by the fact of Nibs's licensing, instead of by a person. How could this be? Jaime gave both his name and his phone number to Animal Control. He was certainly reachable had either Petersen or Yeutter chosen to pursue the person responsible for there being a story in the first place.

Why does it matter? Willy knew immediately why it mattered when he asked: where are the hispános?

It matters because they were written out of the story. Jaime's brother described it not just as an erasure of two men, but as an erasure of an entire ethnic group. Just another manifestation of a system working to exclude people outside of the dominant, white, middle-class cultural narrative. It matters for people inside the dominant cultural narrative, too, not just because of what's lost to all community members when a community isn't inclusive, but because they are the ones directly responsible for the loss, of allowing an exclusive system to function and thrive. What difference would it make if the news story made clear who was responsible for Nibs's rescue? It would make visible people usually rendered invisible by cultural, social, and economic capital. It would celebrate the good deed of someone who doesn't look the same, doesn't do the same kind of work, doesn't sound like Nibs's owner, or like Peterson, or like Steve Beal. And maybe that chips away, just a little, at the us/them myth perpetuated by, well, you know who by now.

Take just a small story, the story of Jamie and Nibs the missing cat. It's an anecdote rich in kindness, humor, and detail coming from Jaime, and a narrative that circles around administration and city income coming from Peterson. I'll tell you Jaime's own words to me as we were talking about this: "Nadie sabe más que yo, porque I find el gato."

No one knows more than me, because I found the cat.

•

When 1011 NOW reframed this narrative to leave out Jaime and Edy, they did more than hide the real story behind Nibs's safe return. A bigger story was also ignored, that of Jaime and his friend working outside in new construction on that snowy winter day. A story that, if anyone would ask, would lead to the discovery that most days of the year are like this, Saturdays and Sundays included: you can find people working and working and working, until the weather makes it impossible (concrete won't set, or won't set properly, below a certain temperature). "Missing Cat" is preoccupied with a pet that could have frozen to death but was rescued and returned to a safe and warm home. That safe and warm home, ironically, was one exactly like those constructed by Jaime and others in his field: hell, the concrete work for that home might even have been done *by* him, in harsh temperatures unfit for cat and human alike.

Jaime's story of Nibs has stuck with me because of how he tells it. Important parts of Jaime's identity, as a construction worker, a Guatemalan, a Hispanic, a migrant, as a nonnative English speaker—apparently these identities aren't encouraged to speak out by gatekeepers like 10 11 NOW. 10 11 NOW showed us this in how they rewrote the story. To Jaime, importantly, the rescue of Nibs stands out in his mind as a good thing he did, an interesting and exciting moment in years and years of doing the same work—but also as a moment that reinforced something he was all too familiar with—the ease with which people take advantage of his work without a glance back.

There are billions of stories to tell. Why didn't we hear Jaime's?

•

By most student and teacher standards, 7:15 a.m. is early, but that's when I walked to class, wanting to arrive in plenty of time to teach at 8:00 a.m. I am a morning person, and further conditioned by work to rise early, so to begin a job at 8:00 a.m. seems late to me.

When I began working at Midnight, I discovered that I could park my pickup in their employee lot and walk to campus easily. For an extra five or ten minutes of walking, I avoided paying hundreds of dollars a semester for parking. I also discovered that several of the guys I worked with would offer me rides to school when they could. Sam frequently gave me a ride in the morning, saying he never had any kids, so this was like taking a daughter to school. Tacks rushed over to pick me up when it was raining, and my bicycle too. Mateen, heading home for the evening, gathered me up upon seeing me walking through the lot on my way back to campus for a night class. It felt like a close network of uncles and brothers, giving me a lift both physically and mentally to make sure I got to class, to make sure I kept going.

But when I walked, the route to Andrews Hall took me past the engineering building on the edge of campus, under construction to make it bigger, better, and shinier (literally true, the construction has added a brilliant glass walkway connecting one part of the complex to the next). When I sat in my truck at the plant, waiting for my next load, I could see this construction site well. It went on for years. I hauled many loads of concrete there, for footings, for floors, for other structural components I can't name. It is the only jobsite where I've had a true argument with a customer. This was early on in its construction, on a Saturday in early COVID times, when a white man with a complex took issue with me asking him not to touch my truck without gloves. He ran the chutes, red-faced and yelling, while I poured from inside the cab. I couldn't hear the names he called me over the truck noise, but the discomfort on the faces of the other men told me all I needed to know. But that's old history now.

Each time I walked by the engineering jobsite, there were men working. I never saw a woman there. When I walked by, they were not usually pouring concrete, but there were all kinds of other work happening. Men driving telehandlers designed to reach and lift, pallets and metal boxes carefully balanced on the forked ends. Men welding steel to steel. Men climbing and balancing, tying rebar, building frames. I walked down the 16th Street sidewalk in my dress clothes, good jeans or maybe a skirt, sweater or a button-down print, leather shoes with a slight heel, loaded down with a backpack, my lunch bag, another bag with more books. I walked by and looked at the men working in their hard hats, jeans, their boots, their hi-vis T-shirts layered under more hi-vis safety vests. After class, I would rush back to Midnight and perform my Clark Kent routine in the women's bathroom, putting on those same clothes.

I looked at the men working, and I felt something every time.

I felt like calling out, although they wouldn't know me, although they might recognize me up close as the lady concrete driver. I looked at them and I became suddenly uncomfortable in the clothes I was wearing, in where I was going, in what I was about to do, because seeing the men work, watching this world unfold in front of me while I was not a part of it was unsettling. In my teacher/student clothes, I felt disguised. In another world entirely, dressed up like a person who does an entirely different thing, lives an entirely different life. I felt like an impostor. I felt phony. I was and am a great teacher, but I was not in my own body in that moment as I saw my other world across the street. I felt this and I always walked on, anxious now, no matter how early and prepared I was.

I felt like I couldn't claim the other, important work that I did.

Not many on campus knew, but my mark as a mixer truck driver was all over that institution. One of my first on-campus pours happened during my first summer at Midnight. It was right outside the English department, replacing a section of curb and sidewalk. I was so giddy with the coincidence that I had Sam, who was there pouring for the electric company, take a photo of me next to Spike, which is what I named truck 126, the truck I drove every day at the time. Since then, I have poured sections of heated parking lot outside the Institute for Ethnic Studies. I have poured a wheelchair ramp and long sidewalk outside of the administration building. That engineering building. Many, many yards of concrete have gone to the new teachers' college. I have poured concrete around outside light fixtures, around new electric car charging stations. I have poured more footings, more floors, more parking lots, more fixtures for the sports arena, and I have poured concrete grout into underground pipes to fill in the ground to support a new track. I have poured a lot of these same things on the university's Innovation Campus for a new hotel, including days spent pouring into hole after hole after hole made by the biggest drill I've ever seen. Pour after pour for the new Lutheran student center. I've poured concrete for renovations at a frat house, for new sidewalks and paving outside the alumni center. I've poured outside the Sheldon Art Museum, anchors for new sculpture installations.

I've never listed all the things I've poured until now, and I'm astounded at the number. Doubtless I've forgotten a few. I've poured a few times for I don't know what, the concrete put into a loader and carried off to a location I couldn't see. We are pouring now a new addition to the football stadium (yet another new perk for the football team), in its early stages, still only footings and walls.

And our most recent university work: a busy corner on the edge of campus. I don't know what it will be, but undoubtedly something for science or business. The jobsite engulfs what was an old parking lot and part of a street. In the early stages of construction, I didn't take notice of what was happening, too busy trying to get around it and down to at the job at the engineering college.

Then one day I am given a load to this new job, and when I pull up to it, I am shocked that part of the street is completely gone, totally gone, earth and everything. I'm staring at a massive hole in the ground. A few weeks later, I drive purposefully into the hole. We pour seventy yards of concrete (seven trucks' worth) into footings, shimmying down a steep dirt ramp to get into the hole, tight, not much room to turn to get out. I stand deep down in this crater and look up to the surrounding campus. Cars driving by, students crisscrossing the streets on the way back to dorms and Greek houses. I think about all the things I've poured for UNL and how this is one of the most striking. Down here, I can see the exposed foundation of the building next door. At one time, other workers poured that foundation, only for it to be buried, unseen and forgotten, part of the process. I crane my neck up at the sky and the activity above and think about how the work we are doing in this hole will also be hidden by whatever will get plopped on top. Before I started as a concrete driver, I had no idea about footings, about foundations that ran so deep into the ground to hold these buildings up. What we are doing down here will all be buried, the hole filled in, the street repaved, our work invisible. I will be able to walk by later and know I poured the footing for that building, but only I will know.

•

It is 6:00 a.m. at Midnight Concrete and all the Laforte Street crew, drivers and yard laborers and the site supervisor, sit dutifully in the plastic chairs lined up in careful rows in the open space adjacent to the breakroom. We have been called to a meeting, which I've been told is about COVID (still in its early days), and I am expecting to see someone from the management team or the corporate office.

But as we all get settled in and the chatter dies down, I notice there's no one unusual in sight. No one that doesn't belong here. So who's running this meeting? Looking exhausted, Malachi tells us this will be a conference call instead, and as he struggles to connect to the call through the newly installed smart TV mounted to the wall, I understand that all drivers and yard crews are gathered at their individual plants to hear this message. The problem here is that Malachi can't make the call play on the TV, so he says we'll have to listen to it through his cell phone. This seems woefully inadequate, and one of the drivers jogs outside to his truck and grabs a small Bluetooth speaker. Still inadequate, but it's enough I guess, and Malachi balances the little speaker next to the yard crew's time clock.

"Can everybody hear it?"

We can kinda sorta hear it if the air conditioner doesn't kick on. Malachi, a year younger than me, is not in his most positive mood this morning and grumbles and moans about the call, sitting with his arms crossed in a chair behind me and cracking quiet jokes with a few of the guys.

The meeting and the call *are* bullshit, really. The parent company of Midnight invited some doctor from the university medical center to talk to a select group of corporate management about the new strain of COVID. The point is obviously to convince everyone to get vaccinated. What we hear at our "meeting" today is a recording of that initial meeting. The doctor has a lot of credentials and is *someone,* an influencer in the COVID crisis. We are told this explicitly, and it is made obvious when whoever is introducing him reads through a long list of accolades, and the only thing I can remember is that he advised two presidents. Why does any of that matter to us?

And then something interesting happens, the one thing I will take away from this (because the doctor does not end up telling us anything we have not already heard). This disembodied company voice from the conference call, by way of contextualizing the speaker's invitation to speak to us, says that these management team members have come together to be proactive about COVID, but when he says it, he doesn't say "managers" or "leadership," oh no, instead he says a phrase I have never heard before:

"A group of thought leaders . . ."

Thought leaders?

This catches my attention and just as I am about to say: "Thought leaders? So what, we're not thought leaders here?"

Malachi says it out loud, right behind me.

# Refrain

A thing I hear truck drivers say.

I know I'm just a dumb truck driver but . . .

    I know I'm just a dumb truck driver but . . .

I know I'm just a dumb truck driver but . . .

    I know I'm just a dumb truck driver but . . .

        I know I'm just a dumb truck driver but . . .

I know I'm just a dumb truck driver but . . .

    I know I'm just a dumb truck driver.

# **Schooled**

An irony of Jaime's story is that journalists are trained to go out and *find* stories, which confirms what I've always been taught: that important narratives come from others, from the community. Jaime possessed a story, and 1011 NOW, perhaps naively, but powerfully, overlooked it. Centering their own narratives, they offer viewers nothing original. This is much like what Martin Eden discovers about his sheltered girlfriend, who is unable to think outside of what she has been taught, unable to look beyond her own limited surroundings. London writes in his novel: "She had read about it, studied about it, in the university in the course of earning her Bachelorship of Arts; but she was not original, not creative, and all manifestations of culture on her part were but harpings of the harpings of others." A key scene in *Martin Eden* shows Martin and his girlfriend enjoying a pleasant day reading poetry together, but when they talk about the poems, they discover their understandings of them differ: "It was beyond her to realize that, out of his experiences of men and women and life, his interpretations were far more frequently correct than hers." From living life as a sailor, rather than reading and studying about it, Martin has accumulated a vast corpus of knowledge that functions both in the "real world" and equally well when applied to interpreting the Romantic poets.

But lived experience and working knowledge get devalued when compared to "education." In the academic context students who come from poor or working-class homes find reification in the university of what they've experienced in many forms leading up to their entrance in the college classroom: that how they speak, how they think, or where they come from isn't good enough. This message will be implicit, or sometimes not, but it will be there. That is quite a burden for one's identity. Additionally, the students we teach, because they are in the privileged space of the classroom, are likely to become the gatekeepers in the future, the dispensers of "culture" and fact, the Steve Beals and Abbie Petersens of the community. It is little wonder then that Jaime never got a chance to speak to 1011 NOW: what value could a construction worker's words have?

Across time, ethnicity, gender, sexuality, and geography, many have questioned what knowledge is and who the keepers of knowledge really are, writing from personal experience and reassuring us: you are not alone. After immigrating from Russia and growing up poor in New York, Anzia Yezierska wrote *Bread Givers* (1925), where protagonist Sara Smolinsky finally attends college after working at a laundry to pay her own way. After a psychology teacher challenges the class to volunteer personal examples to support the textbook, Sara is the first to jump to her feet. The opportunity to relate her own experience, which she can do easily, is just what Sara needs to kickstart her comprehension of psychology: "In a few weeks I was ahead of anyone else in the class. I saw the students around me as so many pink-faced children who never had to live yet. I realized that the time when I sold herring in Hester Street, I was learning life more than if I had gone to school." I've done this too; my hand shot up in the air just a few weeks ago when a professor asked for "real-life examples" of a critical point, and my trucking stories served me well again, as they so often have.

In Richard Wright's novel *Native Son* (1940), a short exchange between Bigger and his friend Gus demonstrates how desire and aptitude are hindered by class and race barriers:

"I *could* fly a plane if I had a chance," Bigger said.

"If you wasn't black and if you had some money and if they'd let you go to that aviation school, you *could* fly a plane," Gus said.

For a moment Bigger contemplated all the 'ifs' that Gus had mentioned. They both broke into hard laughter . . .

*Beyond the Pale*, a 2013 novel by Elana Dykewomon, has Chava Meyer thinking about the ways in which gender is used to bar women's knowledge, of any variety, from books and a broader audience:

I wondered if they read Yiddish authors at Henry Street or only goyim. Either way it was always men, men who were remembered for what they wrote. Maybe in the new world things could still be different, and women would be remembered too. No one remembered working girls—was that why women had children, so someone would remember us?"

And it is (hopefully) obvious, what Barbara Ehrenreich writes, that "Low-wage workers are no more homogeneous in personality or ability than people who write for a living, and no less likely to be funny or bright. Anyone in the educated classes who thinks otherwise ought to broaden their circle of friends."

•

At 4:30 a.m. I stand next to my truck. It is summer, early, dark. We are all here, us drivers, waiting inside our growling trucks to load, or having loaded already, on our way to an early pour. I have just pulled my truck out from under the plant, fully loaded with ten and a half yards of concrete. I climb out and down, pulling on my gloves, walking to the back of the truck to spray off stray concrete blobs, to flip over my flop-over chute before I pull out into the public street. At the back of the truck I pause, looking up. Across the street is an unobtrusive building, bland, the corporate office of our parent company. I didn't know it for the longest time, but there is where the president sits, the owner, the CEO and CFO and whoever else. The family, father and son. The payroll folks, human resources. At 4:30 a.m. every single window is dark. I look at the corner window, the one closest to where I stand next to my truck. The office of the man himself, the man responsible for all of this. The big window is dark. What time will they all arrive? What time does he arrive? 7:00? 8:00? Even later? Hours from now.

•

Do you believe me when I tell you that there's a lot to know about concrete, never mind that there's also a lot to know about being a good truck driver? I am an experienced truck driver, but when I started the job at Midnight, I knew nothing about concrete except that it hardens and fast. I had never hauled concrete before. And over the course of the summer, every day, I was reminded of what a dummy I was in this arena, watching construction crews work with this stuff, learning more about the ins and outs of hauling it from experienced mixer drivers, discovering there actually was a science to the making of concrete, as well as many different types and mixes, all of it. There's a lot to know. A lot to know.

It is physical work, of course. Can we count it as intellectual labor?

Most would not think of construction workers as practitioners of intellectual labor. Yet truck drivers, construction crews, and concrete finishers all possess highly specific knowledge of their trade. That they work in what we call a "trade" doesn't imply an absence of smarts, but it's a different kind of knowledge than an "intellectual" has. Academics are these so-called intellectuals and are trained to be knowledgeable in a particular academic field and subfield. Is that really so different from a concrete finisher?

In many obvious ways, yeah. You can get trained pretty cheaply to lay concrete: just get someone to give you a job, then show up with a good attitude and a few cheap tools. It is easy work to access, with little or no formal education. And of course, construction work doesn't hold the cultural cachet that being a professor does, and with that comes a large power differential.

But when we say intellectual work, do we mean something different, more general, perhaps just the capacity for deep thinking? What is that, exactly? And how could we ever know from the outside who does it and who doesn't? And why am I so bound up in choosing one over the other? Perhaps because intellectualism is prioritized in this country, or at least prioritized by intellectuals and others intent on keeping the status quo. Several of my coworkers are extremely supportive of my graduate education, admiring my (according to them) accomplishments and drive. But there are also many times I get rolling about a book or theory, and they look at me like I just landed from space. I could read that as a lack of comprehension on their part. Or I could read it as bemusement. Or something else. To answer questions about this divide between physical and intellectual work, we must be willing to implicate ourselves and admit, for example, that discussing novels might in many contexts be quite ridiculous to people whose waking hours are spent laboring in order to earn a wage to survive.

Because there are perceived rewards that come with a college degree, many of us wind up there, pushed by parents or driven by need to see what we can make of ourselves, see if we can "do better." We might, as I generally do, even enjoy schooling, not suspecting for a minute that the role we play as teachers and advocates of university education might not be the noble pursuit it seems (it comes, I think, at great personal cost to really consider this, to implicate yourself in this way, at something you've invested so much of your life into). This isn't to say that we shouldn't learn, but only that there might be other ways to do so.

I am not only arguing that trade work is intellectual. Laborers participate in similar kinds of intellectualism through their real-time experiencing of the very things—issues relating to ethnicity and gender—we discuss and unpack in the classroom. In my trucker life, I witness these issues play out right in front of me, every day. We live them. I've seen and listened to my coworkers: my compadres, my friends, my brothers and uncles and sisters, my Black, Latino, and Kurdish coworkers tell tales of the shit they deal with all the time.

The problem is that sitting in the classroom sometimes prevents one from seeing it. When you are on the receiving end of constant abuse, you can talk quite intelligently about it yourself (even though, in this context, some might not think of it as theorizing). When I talk about the books I've read that deal with racism or marginalization, many men I work with understand it perfectly; they have a lifetime of information to share on the subject. So here is the same type of intellectual labor, being exchanged at places many consider lacking in such activity. How many breakroom conversations have I witnessed, its participants navigating the choices of what-to-do and how-to-deal after another incident of a racial slur, bullying, objectification?

Quite a few.

•

When one of my students contextualizes her question about the value of education by sharing that about half of her high school friends went straight to work after high school, and that the other half are in college, I answer the question as best I can, and then end by telling her and her peers that, every day, she's leaving those high school friends behind. You are leaving them behind, I say without budging. You are on a path that is going to put distance between you and them, simply by you being in this classroom, whether you know it or not. It seems like a cruel thing to tell a nineteen-year-old, but crueler still would be to pretend I don't know that it will take much active work on her part to maintain those friendships. I speak to her from my experience, and from evidence I see in stories all around me. Cultural critic Ivan Illich writes from a different time and context, where the chasm between the schooled and unschooled ran even deeper:

> The university graduate has been schooled for selective service among the rich of the world. Whatever his or her claims of solidarity with the Third World, each American college graduate has had an education costing an amount five times

greater than the median life income of half of humanity. A Latin American student is introduced to this exclusive fraternity by having at least 350 times as much public money spent on his education as on that of his fellow citizens of median income. With very rare exceptions, the university graduate from a poor country feels more comfortable with his North American and European colleagues than with his nonschooled compatriots, and all students are academically processed to be happy only in the company of fellow consumers of the products of the educational machine.

On the one hand, school funnels its graduates directly into the service of capitalism, and school itself is a branch of that machine that produces a never-ending need for consumption. We know the certification that university graduates receive from having been educated puts them on an economic path that is different from nonschooled peers, and if it doesn't immediately provide an economic return, it provides a safety net allowing more opportunity and flex to find that return as a person progresses through life. But perhaps more importantly, Illich argues that the very existence of schools works a negative psychological effect on those who cannot or choose not to attend:

> Everywhere, all children know that they were given a chance, albeit an unequal one, in an obligatory lottery, and the presumed equality of the international standard now compounds their original poverty with the self-inflicted discrimination accepted by the dropout. They have been schooled to the belief in rising expectations and can now rationalize their growing frustration outside school by accepting their rejection from scholastic grace.

It is something I see reflected everywhere, this split. My own best friend from high school, a brilliant and creative woman who tried both the university and community college after high school graduation, repeatedly dropping out, has waitressed in a keno restaurant for most of her adult life. She keeps her distance now, confessing embarrassment about her economic and familial restraints. My own academic loneliness is exacerbated by not being able to talk to my father about what I am doing; it is not that he does not want to talk, but that we are speaking different languages. When I asked him if he knew what a dissertation was, I was surprised that he did, and he proceeded to define it light-heartedly as "some long b.s. paper that no one ever reads." I can understand why he feels the way he does. My dissertation adviser, a first-generation college student, has told me similar things about talking with her madre, and I see this story reflected in the work of many professors who've guided me. I see it in the front of my very own English department, one floor down from my office, just outside by the steps on the east side of the building, one August day as I am pouring concrete for a new sidewalk.

•

Yes, that's right, I am in my concrete truck, pouring sidewalk just feet from my very own building, a few weeks before the start of my final year in school.

The job is for thirty yards of concrete, and I am the second truck on the scene. I drive south down 14th Street from Vine until the street runs out and ends in a small circle. I drive up and over the curb and down the wide sidewalk that runs between the quad and the greenspace next to the library. After beginning the job near the place where the two library buildings intersect, I still have some concrete left in my truck. So we back down the same sidewalk we came in on, finishing the pour just under the tree outside Andrews Hall that shades students as they walk to and from my classes. Later I will discover that I can look out my office window, turn my head to the left, and see my little patch of concrete.

The closeness of my concrete truck and the English department is too much for me to handle. I badly want to take a picture of the two together. But I am not the last truck on the job, and I've got to move my truck to the street to wash my chutes and make room for Ryan to pour. I content myself with the thought that I already have a picture (for I had poured in almost this same spot two years before) when something serendipitous happens. The leader of the crew pouring the concrete walks over and asks me if they can use my water hose to wash their equipment. I think he wants me to wait in the street, but he asks if I can move the truck right next to the fresh concrete. I aim 138 right at the English department, drive up over the curb, and set the brakes a few feet from the east steps of Andrews.

The crew leader, whose name I have never asked but soon will (it's Alan), takes the hose from the back of my truck and sprays their power buggy, and then wets the concrete we have just poured. I am always a little intimidated by Alan, for he is reserved and gruff and barked at me on my first job for him. This is why I've never asked his name. He is about my age and has a single ear pierced, a look that reminds me of the early nineties. But on this day, Alan or not, having my truck practically kissing Andrews Hall makes me bold. Cell phone in hand, I approach Alan.

I smile. "Ummm, I was wondering, could you please take a picture of me and my truck in front of the building? I go to school here," I say, pointing, "and my office is right up there."

"You go to school here?" he asks. Many of the customers I chat with know this, but as I said, Alan mostly communicated by grunting to me. I nod my assent. "For what?"

"For my PhD in English."

I have his attention. "You want to be a teacher or something?"

"Well . . . I did. Now I'm not so sure it's the right thing for me anymore," I say, my pervasive honesty making me talkative. "Since I've been out here working, my perspective has changed a little."

Alan grins and a laugh bursts out. "I understand that! They don't have any idea what goes on out here in the real world." He shakes his head, still smiling. I laugh along with him.

"So can you take my picture?"

"You're serious? Okay." I hand him my phone, turn on my heel, and jog to the front of the truck. I put my left elbow on the left fender of my guy, 138, and smile. Alan snaps the picture. In it, my boots are together, left knee bent just a little, safety glasses pushed to the top of my head. I am wearing my modified men's hi-vis shirt. I am in violation of the loose dress code because there are holes in the thighs and the knees of my faded jeans where the fabric has worn thin. My right thigh has a huge wet spot on it, where I've been messy while washing my chutes. I have a huge smile on my face. I have always hated pictures of myself.

I love this photo. It is my favorite picture of me.

# Not a Chick

I'm not sure if this guy bugs me because he doesn't smile, or because it seems like he's glaring at me.

I know that I've been conditioned my entire life to smile. Taught to please, to be polite. When the trick doesn't get the result it is designed to, it's like a puzzle waiting to be solved.

Laforte Street sits in a high pedestrian traffic area, across from the university and tucked alongside a neighborhood of old and inexpensive homes and apartments. Strung down the street is a community skateboard center and offbeat artist galleries and workspaces prettily reworked from old industrial buildings. It's an eclectic mix that begets a lot of foot traffic, especially from students or university workers who live nearby or park for free on the neighborhood streets before crossing Meadowlark to enter that other world.

This guy is one of those people I recognize just from walking back and forth, to and from wherever he goes and wherever he comes from. He's young, maybe in his twenties, and looks Middle Eastern if I'd have to guess. He is not tall and is pear shaped, with thick dark hair, a short beard, and a perpetually furrowed brow.

I am not always in a hurry, but often I am, and damn it if people just don't walk so slow. I wait with a veneer of patience in the street to turn into the pit to wash, or to come out of the pit area to park and scramble to eat. I wait for them to cross the driveways of our plant so I can do what I need to do with the truck and grab a few minutes to pee, or chat with my friends, or whatever. I smile at the people from the cab of my truck out of friendliness, or habit, or to mask the desire to yell at them to please hurry the hell up and get out of my way.

And this guy never freaking smiles. I swear he glares at me. I begin to take it personally and start my own private test with him, suppressing my polite smile whenever I catch him crossing my path.

On this particular Tuesday we are just busy as hell. It was the same way yesterday, and it will be the same way, I later discover, all week long. There are no breaks between loads, a new ticket coming across our screens in a minute or less after we arrive back at the plant. Busy, miserably busy.

I clunk over the potholes on 19th Street and approach the driveway that leads to the wash pit, and here's Grumpy today, in his standard polo shirt, backpack strapped on and lolling slowly down the public sidewalk that crosses the pit entrance. I wait, resolute in this moment not to smile. I may have even frowned, so determined I was to play along with his game, to not capitulate with a friendly gesture if he was so resolute to hold firm with this glare. The things you think about after being in a truck all day.

So here I am in 138, frowning at Grumpy and wishing he would speed it up a notch so I can get a minute to rest. He makes eye contact with me, then looks back down at the ground.

And then a remarkable thing happens. He pulls his elbows up and his forearms in to do a little jog across the drive. He speeds up, and then, so help me, looks up at me again and gives me a hesitant, half smile. And *then*, and of all things, he says, "I'm sorry I'm so slow!"

My window is down so I lean out as he clears my path and I turn into the driveway. "It's okay!" I shout. "Have a good day!"

He is already past me and clearly doesn't know whether to stop, or whether I will stop, or what to do. I don't know either. We do one of those awkward jerky hesitant things, me in the truck and him on the ground, and then he turns and I just stop, truck butt out on the street but who cares, and I lean farther out the window as he turns around and approaches the truck.

"Do you do other things around here or do you drive this truck?" he asks. I smile because, well, I am sitting in the truck as he asks this, have *been* sitting in the truck, driving it, every time he's ever glanced up at me from under those brows.

Playfully then, I say, "Well, I can do anything around here. But yes, I drive this truck all the time."

"And they allow you to do that?"

I wonder what my face must have looked like. It must have taken a moment for me to recover. Yet surprised as I am, I am not surprised at all. "Why do you ask?" I reply.

"Well, I just don't see chicks driving trucks."

I stare.

He's done it again, twice now, confounded me with a particular word choice. "Allow" and "chicks": my mind is at a loss.

I get it together and say, "Look, first of all, I'm a woman, not a chick." He is serious and just gazes at me. "And yes, there's quite a few of us that drive." I am still smiling, and he continues a serious gaze and nods, beginning to turn away.

"And another thing," I lean out the window and sort of wave my arm. "I do it better than most of the guys." He is beginning to take a step away and I let off the clutch and ease into the accelerator, creeping forward and away, astonished at this interaction, astonished, mostly, at the word allow.

Later, a few of us get a few precious minutes of rest time between loads. I had already scarfed my food when Bob arrives at the plant, and we find ourselves at the truck drivers' water cooler: the bench outside the plant office. Bob and John sit next to each other and I, unusually animated for a hot midafternoon, lean against the parked maintenance pickup. We talk, and I tell this story to Bob. I tell him about "allowed" and he laughs, but I can see in his face that he too is surprised, that he gets my astonishment about this, which makes me happy.

"You should have had fun with him," Bob says, to which I agree, but I'm not that quick of a thinker. "You should have told him you stole it."

I throw my head back in laughter. "That's good, yeah, like, I'm just driving this until they figure it out, so far no one's noticed me." We laugh and shake our heads, come up with more ideas, and I pace a little, put my elbows up and down, moving, excited, incredulous. We watch the board, and before long my number is up, then John's and Bob's.

I think about this later of course, a little in love with Bob's joke about me stealing a mixer and just driving it. They allow you to do this? Nope, no way, but I let nothing stand in my way, just swiping a mixer truck and hiding in plain sight, hauling loads with the guys until someone notices.

But later, in a more serious moment I think that perhaps Bob is quite right. I've stolen it, haven't it? I am not what they think I am, not what they thought they'd get. Sometimes I am less, and I know I am more. Sometimes I am their perfect driver, following all the rules, forever smiling, them calling me Sunshine. And when I'm not, both less and more in these moments: less because I am not doing what I am supposed to do, I speak up, I don't smile, I repeat again and again the problems I see and what we should do about them, I am a pain en las nalgas, a pain in the ass; and I am more because of all these same things. What have I stolen, in plain sight, from this rough and tumble man's world? What have I taken from them, for myself, and what, I really wonder, or how, have I disrupted the order of things?

Yes, they have allowed me to do this, I guess they have.

# Partnership

He turns the key and the truck's dash lights blink out as 141 shudders to a stillness. The truck gasps as air whooshes and releases, takes one giant sigh before heaving itself downward to settle in for the night.

"I love how my truck groans after I shut him off," Bob says to me. He mimics the conversation between him and 141.

"Like 'Ohhh thank you Bob, finally, I needed that.'"

"No problem old truck," and he gives the fender a pat. "Good job today," as he walks away.

# Craft

"You drive a truck? I could never do that," women often say to me.

"Yes, sure you could," I always say back.

Trucking is not for everyone, same as any job, but it is not *not* for women. We've been pushed away from it, taught that it's men's work since the moment we were born and wrapped up tight in pink blankets, soft pink hats jammed on our newborn heads. From that moment, we've been schooled in what's for us and what isn't.

There's no reason to listen to those voices. I drive a big machine.

And that's what he is, 138, a machine, even though he's more than that, a partner to me, a friend. I know this truck is a very large, very heavy machine with both simple and complex mechanical parts and systems. It was built by someone's hands and can be unbuilt the same way. Operating it is something that's learned. It's practice. It's within my control.

And oh, operating it. Climbing into a truck cab you could collapse under the weight of both power and responsibility. These machines can do damage. They can roll and tumble, smash and push and crumple. They are so much bigger than the majority of vehicles; they are the clear favorite in any shoving match. Diesel engine power, massive tire power, tons of weight power—empty or otherwise—the power of perception as I sit so much higher than you do in your car. With power comes responsibility: I tell driver trainees this and make them face it: in this truck, we'll survive most accidents. The people in cars won't. We can damage so easily, so carelessly. But if you accept that responsibility then you revel in the reward.

Sitting here. Sitting in the truck you are in your own space now, the tiny world around you yours. You are responsible for it. You imagine sometimes, at jobsites, what nondrivers think of the truck and you, your relationship to it. Is it just another part of the day to these construction guys, or are they consciously careful around it, mindful of that power when working so close, within feet of this crushing weight? You are responsible for it, for this truck, so you arrive at work and spend time inspecting: do his tires have enough bounce, is he bleeding coolant or oil, is the air flowing through his veins? You give your truck a pat and a pep talk in the morning and a pat and a thank you as you slide out of the cab at the end of your day. Legally, technically, he's not yours but he might as well be.

Drivers are defined by the movement of their trucks, their loads. But the weird thing is that when it comes to moving, drivers do and we don't. Bear with me. Sure, I cross miles of ground every day in a truck, but while I'm doing that, I'm sitting pretty snugly in the cab of 138. It's warm, the seat is comfortable-ish, I can stretch out my legs if I put the seat on the floor, and the music choices are mine for the making. For twelve-ish hours a day, this is my home, my office, my nest. It smells like La Chica Fresita air freshener in here. The truck moves and I move with it, but I am also very stationary inside it. There's something about being still inside the truck, about driving, moving down the road, that I'm in love with.

Operating a truck when it's moving through the city is far from boring; it's a symphony, an orchestra of movements that sings your talent, your force. When I'm scooting along O Street or cresting Sun Valley Boulevard or patiently idling at the "No Right Turn" arrow at the intersection we nicknamed X, to make all that happen, that's movement, that's skill and power, that's navigation and technique. Any job, any roadway, whether in forward or reverse, is a beautiful coming together of many tiny movements.

*A driver's left foot pushes the clutch all the way down when preparing to stop, but just a little way down when preparing to shift. Her right hand cradles the gearshift, fingers flipping the range selector and arm guiding the shifter from gear to gear. Her hands make constant, tiny adjustments to the steering wheel to keep the vehicle where she wants it, her eyes always scanning for the next potential hazard, her head shifting between left mirror and right, windshield, gauges, then mirrors again. As she moves, her truck moves, synchronized, using every bit of available space to make a tight turn, gliding to the left or right to avoid traffic drifting into her lane . . .*

And these are just the basics, the minimum, the very minute details of operating the machine. Movements become more complicated as scenarios change: heavy urban traffic, icy roads and gusting winds, nightfall. Backing into a customer's jobsite requires an additional set of movements, tiptoeing through a workplace minefield in low low gear. With time and experience, this results in a synchronicity with the truck, me and 138, you and your machine, working it but also working with it, a fluidity of movements that become second nature. Our bodies seem still ensconced inside machines, but there is labor being done at every moment.

Always working.

Shifting. Constantly shifting. Operating the clutch. Or will you float gears? Turning. Head turning with it, where's the ass end?

Backing. I love the challenge of backing and this has been a gift of all the trucking jobs I've had: there are so many opportunities to back up. It is possible to arrive to a concrete job and not immediately have to back, but it's uncommon. The shrill *beep beep beep* of the backup alarm as 138 goes into reverse, we arrive and back everywhere to get the truck where he needs to be, which means dodging countless land mines, small and large, missing deep holes where footings have been dug, squeezing into spaces with inches to spare on either side, looking up too so you don't rip down an awning or an alley power line, seeing the satisfaction of the customer when you put your truck farther along than he had expected you'd be able to.

No one can take my driving away from me, no one can take away what I can do or the skill I have, what I can show with that skill, even if it goes unacknowledged. As workers, drivers don't produce anything tangible (like construction workers and countless others, we can't point to one concrete object we have individually crafted), but observation reveals the evidence of the craftsmanship. A CDL is special; not everyone will learn this skill. Being able to drive is not the same as being an excellent driver: a truck driver. That we do this thing and others don't, that we operate equipment that others can't. When the guys in the polo shirts tell you in the safety meeting that this business couldn't run without you, you feel flattered, but—there's more than one type of power in that. Think about it. They really couldn't do it without you.

An orchestra of tiny, beautiful movements each person learns and adapts to make the craft her own. Tiny, beautiful movements that power machines, tiny, beautiful movements to navigate this world.

# What We Might Do

I imagine what it would be like to have the five women drivers spread across four different plants all working from the same location.

If there were five of us, we'd be almost half of the driver force at Laforte.

If there were five of us, a woman wouldn't be the exception.

We wouldn't all agree, we might not like each other. But we'd be half of the bodies, different bodies. Fifty percent more opportunity for a different perspective. Fifty percent harder to ignore our presence.

It might be us taking up all the space on the one bench outside the breakroom, instead of Luis, with his long arm stretched out and long legs splayed and his buddies and little brother hanging off his every word, sucking the air.

Would there be a new clique, or less cliques?

Would Midnight have to adjust the bathroom situation so there was more than one women's stall? Would we need to remodel?

Would I know firsthand the problems Rena had at a jobsite, instead of the hearsay I'd come to months later? Would I approach my customers differently, knowing they smiled at me but gave Kate a bunch of shit?

What would I learn from Debbie that I could never learn from Matt or Ratt?

If we were working from one plant, all dispatched to the same big job, what would it be like to have five women present, five women in the same space, five women disrupting, five women powerful, five women showing off and doing it just as good or better, five women making this normal . . . what would it be like . . .

I wonder. I wonder if Rena and Josie and Kate and Debbie and I were assigned to different plants intentionally. Coincidence? Or recognition from the management of what could happen, what *could be*? A clue, a tell, a fear, perhaps, that they know perfectly well, that we women could upset the whole orderly conduct of life.

I wonder.

## Parts of Speech

Before Midnight, before concrete, I poured.

    I poured my coffee each morning.

        I poured myself into my studies.

            I poured my heart out at inappropriate moments and I poured myself into fictional worlds.

But when I arrived at my concrete life, oh, how I poured.

*To pour, a verb:*

    We pour concrete when it leaves the truck and is placed on the ground.

        We pour basements, patios, sidewalks, foundations, slabs of all sizes and uses.

            We are pouring,

we were pouring,

we will pour 500 yards on that 4:00 a.m. job tomorrow.

*Pour, a noun:*

We can be "on the job" but can just as easily say "on a pour"

or "that pour over there,"

or "you know that pour on South 27th Street?"

I poured, we poured, when you were pouring. I like to pour basements with a pump truck, and sometimes with chutes 'cause it's more interesting, but only if I can trust the guy.

In Spanish we can use the verb "poner." To put. Estoy poniendo. Voy a poner dos sotanos hoy, if Midnight will give me concrete.

Or, in Spanish you might also use "tirar." To throw, and puedes tirar concreto just as easily as you can pour it.

We pour.

# Uniform

The first time I pour for T&T Concrete, we are in Valparaiso, a tiny village north of Lincoln. The town is eight blocks wide and eight blocks long, my delivery address on the very eastern edge, where the blacktop literally runs out. From the intersection of Fourth and Cleveland, everything I see looks quiet and average: houses, driveways, yards, all well established. Where was the pour? Before heading through the intersection, where the road dead-ended two houses down, I park the truck and get out and look. Sometimes it's better to walk a little on the front end of things.

As I get closer to the address, I see it, new construction in the backyard. There's a giant machine shed going up, for a shop or garage, to park a camper or a tractor or a boat. The house and the neighboring house had obscured my view from the street. As I get closer, the concrete work we'll do is now obvious, and I see men working, men's black pickups parked nearby, men with black T-shirts, men I've never poured for before. What I don't immediately see is how they want me to get my truck to the place we'll be pouring; I don't see any access from the street. I walk closer to the men working, closer still, and stop.

The guy closest to me is white, maybe late-thirties, beefy. He pauses what he's doing and looks up.

"Yeah, can I help you?" He is hastily tying rebar, last-minute.

I look down at my orange hi-vis and my boots. I look up at him. "I wasn't sure how you wanted me to get the truck back here . . . ?"

His eyes shoot back up at me and then over, him craning his neck toward to street to look for a truck. It's obvious then. He had no idea I was the concrete driver.

By that time I've seen there's a way in through a field in the back, I'll just have to drive north a block and enter off Cleveland. I gesture toward the north, looking to confirm my plan with this man, and he nods: "Yeah, back all the way in from the street and we'll buggy it."

I back all the way in from the street. We buggy it. The first time I pour for T&T Concrete, I somehow don't notice their uniforms. Maybe they weren't wearing them, maybe I was just new enough that I was preoccupied with not messing up my job. Maybe I was too focused on the pickups they were driving: shiny black Dodges with big expensive tires, dressed up to show off first, and to work second.

The second time I pour for T&T Concrete, it is a year later, and I roll my eyes inwardly when I get out of my truck, and the owner, the same dude who misplaced me a year before gives me a slow "Wuzzzz uuuup" Beavis and Butthead style. It is not an ill-fitting allusion. He has his hard-hat worn purposefully backward and he is leaning on my truck fender, waiting for me to get back there and put all three chutes on.

The second time I pour for T&T Concrete, I see the shirts, I see the uniforms every guy there is wearing. Some are black and some orange, and on the back the shirts say T&T real nice and big, bold, with the phone number underneath. There are words under the phone number, where it would fall on the wearer's lower back. I stare, trying to comprehend what I think I see. The slogan under the phone number:

        "Big or small, we lay them all."

Imagine this happening: A step-by-step guide on how to create customized T-shirts for your business:

1. Dream up a design. This is your business, your brand! What should your shirts look like? What should they say?
2. Call the screen printer. Explain your design. Be specific, be very clear.
3. Review and confirm your order. Yes, my business name is this. Yes, our phone number is this. Yes, underneath, our slogan is this. Repeat it, yes, that's right, big or small . . . yes, repeat it, that's right. That's what I want.
4. When you are emailed a proof, eye it meticulously. Don't want any mistakes, misspellings. Confirm the final order.
5. Write a check for it. Sign your name.
6. Patiently wait the standard two-to-three-week turn-around time. Imagine your custom shirts going to press, in production: ink on fabric, ink on fabric, ink on fabric, ink on fabric. Stamped out over and over, ink on fabric, ink on fabric, ink on fabric, big or small, big or small, big or small, big or small.
7. They've arrived! Shipped to your door. Slice open the box flaps and pull them apart. Filled to capacity with neat piles of larges, XLs, 2XLs. It's a unique smell. They smell artificial; it's the ink.
8. Haul these boxes to work the next morning and toss several shirts to each of your guys. How many, five, six? A

fresh shirt for each workday? Go to work, get dirty, strip off that sweaty shirt and don another, new again, whole again, to do it all over again.

I dwell on this moment most of all, the distribution. What was the reaction of the men you gave these shirts to? Did they laugh? Did they notice? Did they know ahead of time because you brainstormed the clever slogan together? Did the native Spanish speakers on your crew get the play on words? Did anyone protest? Did anyone decline? Did they even give it a second thought? Was it worth it to them because the shirts were free? Did they do it because you were the boss? Was it okay because everyone else was wearing it too?

The third time I pour for T&T Concrete I am irate before I even leave the plant for the job. I had only seen them twice in as many years, I hadn't expected to see them again. The thought of this—big or small, we lay them all—has me so mad that I have trouble focusing on the route to the job. I am almost blind with what I feel inside of me. All the way there, a continuous loop of feminist arguments, my own feelings, and a simple incredulity at how such a blatantly misogynist artifact is condoned plays in my head. What would things be like when I arrived? Would they still have those shirts?

Yes, yes of course they still have those shirts. We are on the south end of Lincoln and mercifully, it is a pump job, so my interaction with the customer is minimal. When this same dude approaches my truck to tell me to add water to the load I do so silently, speaking only with a sneer.

I stand there and pour and am angry. I stand there and pour and am disgusted. An hour ago I was having a normal day, and now, I know from experience, that's over. I will feel like this for the duration of my workday. I will feel like this when I go home. I will feel and feel and feel and wonder about how little a woman matters in this world.

I will not do this again.

Big or small, we lay them all. Where do I fall on that spectrum?

I pour. Then I climb into my cab and shut the door. I scroll through my phone and find dispatch's number, press it. Jerry answers.

My voice shakes. Anger? Hesitancy to ask for something for myself?

"Hi Jerry. Listen, um, please don't send me back to this customer again. Not today, not in the future."

"Why, what's going on, did something happen?" I hear the concern in his voice.

Will this make sense to him? "No one said anything to me," I say quickly. I hate asking for things. "It's what they're *wearing*." I am gaining steam. "What's on their shirts is disrespectful to women and I'm not going to stand here and see that every time I pour." My voice rises in pitch.

Jerry is by nature quiet. I hear nothing on the phone, for a moment. Then, "What do they say?" He corrects himself almost immediately, his usual stutter, "I guess it doesn't matter." I am glad he knows this.

I tell him what they say. There is a groan, and silence. He doesn't need it explained. "It's okay," he says, "I understand. And we won't send you back. I'll make a note of it here, but if someone forgets, because it's hard to keep track of everything, and you see the load come up, call us and let us know."

I sit there and nod in my truck. "Thank you," I repeat, amazed at how easy this went. "Thank you for understanding."

"Of course," Jerry finishes, "If we don't have any other trucks to send, there might be a time when you have to haul a load."

I sit there and nod, looking out at the parking lot in front of me. I understand.

And it does happen again, once or twice a year, three times, too often. In the parking lot at Laforte, waiting, a load comes up on my board and I look: T&T. Not today, not ever. Each time I call dispatch on the radio. I do not care if there are other trucks in the lot or not. I do not care if that customer waits: "138 to Midnight . . . I don't go to this customer. You'll have to give me something else." Each time one of my comrades flies by in his truck, clunking and thunking over the bumps in the lot, flying by to take my place in line and load this one for me, without complaint, even though they don't know what it's all about, even though it costs them a few minutes of free time. I've explained it to Mateen, and tell him why I make sure to know where I'm going before I back under the plant: "Because, if they start loading me with their load before I catch it, well, then what am I going to do?'

"You put someone else in your truck," Mateen says without hesitancy. That easy. My friend.

Eventually there are rumors, of course, there are always rumors. My request not to go to a customer was not standard practice, for me or anyone else. I hesitated to say anything on the radio where any driver from any plant could hear. Other drivers speculate. I hear once that I don't go to T&T because "they were talking about you in Spanish, and you know Spanish and heard what they were saying, and that's why." That's never happened, not ever, I correct. When T&T loads continue to appear on my board, I become bolder and clearer, saying their name on the radio for all to hear, more emphatic, give me another load, I say, I won't go here. I announce that drivers are welcome to ask me why, if they have questions, knowing that they do, but that they probably won't. I want Katelyn to hear me refuse a load because I don't have to do anything someone else wants, because being an employee doesn't mean giving up all of myself. I want *anyone* who has a problem at a customer to hear me refuse the load, to stand firm. I want anyone who doesn't have trouble with a customer to know that some of us do.

I fantasize about getting a T&T load when there are no trucks in the lot except mine, no one arriving to swoop in and take this one as I make my stand with 138 frozen to the ground. I dream of the customer calling in, furious, wanting to know why he's waiting on trucks, and dispatch telling him that the available truck won't be hauling his load because she doesn't pour for misogynist douchebags. The better, more beautiful dream is that the dispatchers at Midnight tell the stupid customer that he won't be getting more concrete from us, ever, or at least until the shirts disappear, because Midnight supports and values its employees and stands up against disrespect to women, or anyone else.

Why am I still dreaming?

•

It is the beginning of my third summer pouring concrete. Still winter really, but spring fever has caught, and the winter freeze, the massive snowfall, it's all melting and thawing. I climb up on the back of my truck. Where I stand is less than four feet off the ground, but from here I can look down into the concrete chute than runs into the hopper of the pump truck. Here, I can better match the speed of the truck's drum to the speed of the pump once we begin pouring. Only four feet off the ground, but I have a bird's eye view.

We are on a large jobsite, an addition to a pharmaceutical complex that manufactures all sorts of animal-related drugs, and because it is a large jobsite all the standard PPE is required: hard hat, safety glasses, hi-vis. From my pedestal on the truck fender I look down over everything: the pump truck operator and the quality control guy, the jobsite supervisor and the other workers, the giant hole in the ground where we are pouring the concrete footing that day. People come and go. As I ready myself to bring the concrete up when asked, I look down to see that the only one near me was the pump operator, Tony—or is it Tony? With his coat hood up, stocking hat on, hard hat on over that, winter coat, dark safety glasses . . . and a winter beard like most of the guys, he is indistinguishable from other men to me. I think it's Tony, which is important, because although we've had our awkward moments, we're past that stuff now and I like chatting with him. But I don't recognize that hard hat as his: does he have more than one? This one is brown and covered in stickers, and not the job-related kind either, but the smart-ass funny, assert your personality kind that say things like "I'm ready for the shit show" or "Sorry, I don't speak idiot."

A round sticker catches my attention. It is the golden McDonald's arches on a red background; most of the other stickers were black and white. The arches are pasted dead center on the left side of Tony's hard hat. From my post I have an ideal, top-down view.

I can't help but notice those arches: something is different about them. I squint, focusing to look a little closer. Then I want to unsee them, because they aren't arches at all. The joke is on me. What look like arches, are *supposed* to look like arches, are actually a woman's legs, spread, knees in the air where the tips of the arch would typically be, and a silhouette of high heels at the end of the "feet."

I feel sick to my stomach.

Let me not fail to mention the detail meant to complete the optical trick. Under the image is the McDonald's slogan: "I'm lovin' it."

I crawl off of my truck and back to the ground. I stand there and look up at Tony. We are waiting on the others. Is it Tony? I don't know for sure, which tempers what I think I will say to him. I open my mouth: "You know . . ." Slight pause. "That sticker on your hard hat makes me really sad."

Sad? What am I saying?

"What sticker?" The guy who might be Tony pulls his hard hat off and looks at it. "What, McDonald's?" he says, the slight surprise in his voice mixed with amusement. He knows. Funny how he knows just which sticker, of a dozen or two, I am referring to.

"Whatever." I turn away to pull myself back up to the refuge that is my truck fender. We are still only a few feet from one another, but it is a symbolic distance to express my displeasure, or maybe it is just space I need.

That little distance between us doesn't help me. Tony looks at me, and I turn away and stare at my truck, at the concrete churning in the truck's drum, at whatever. I am grateful for dark safety glasses that hide my eyes. Is the awkwardness as palpable as I think it is? My stomach is churning, my thoughts are blurring, my focus is lost as my heart beats faster with this new, completely unexpected moment of anxiety. Does Tony feel it too, or is he just looking at me like he always looks at me?

That sticker, that stupid sticker, draws my eyes toward it although I want to look anywhere else. The only real detail is the outline of the calves and the high heels, just enough shape to make those arches into legs, but I can see it there, in the place where the two arches meet, right above the "I'm lovin' it,": the ready, made-to-order, oh-so-consumable vagina. Or should I call it something else, what it is inevitably called on a jobsite when I am out of earshot. The vagina between those spread legs is in my imagination, but there it is, just right there, conjured in just the way this simple sticker is supposed to conjure it.

The crew on the job are finally ready. The pump gears up and we pour the load. I stay with my truck, watching the concrete, adjusting the speed of the flow and stopping it when the pump stops, starting it when the pump starts. The footings are a hundred feet from me, and Tony is there, operating the pump by the remote-control unit strapped to his waist. The minutes pass as the concrete empties from my truck into his pump truck. I have a decision to make. What will I do from here? Anything? What a child I am, I tell myself, for replying with "Whatever." That's all I could come up with? It wasn't, of course, but it was just all I could speak in that moment in the fever of disgust and anger I felt.

When I am out of concrete, the pump stops, and Tony makes his way back to his truck and mine. I scrape the remaining concrete from my chute into his hopper. I am almost done. I desperately want Tony to open a conversation with me, to say something about this so I won't have to. I will it to happen in my mind. Say something, Tony, so I know this is important to you. Say something so I know you can see this is important to me. Say something so I know that you can see me.

There are other trucks waiting to unload. Pump trucks allow two concrete trucks to be positioned at the hopper at the same time, but because of the landscape at this jobsite, there is only space for one. I will have to move before another truck can back up. While this is happening, work on the footing will stop: no truck at the pump, no concrete.

I know my answer to Tony, my whatever, was just as lousy as that sticker. I know I will kick myself for a very long time if I say nothing better than "whatever." I know it's not my job to educate Tony on sexism, but I can't afford to let the moment pass. We can't afford it. I'm tired. I don't want to talk, shouldn't have to. But I'm *tired*. And it isn't just about me.

I climb down from my truck. Slowly, still thinking. The snow is just melting into a spring, and it is so muddy; the jobsite, without enough gravel, is just a wreck of mud. Tony is there as I climb down; I stand opposite of him, two feet away, looking up at him just a little now that I am back on the ground. So muddy, my two feet are stuck where I stand. I lift one foot with great effort, put it back into place, then the other, putting it back into place, doing a half-conscious dance of indecision, still, I think, waiting for him to speak.

And the jobsite is waiting on me.

"Can I just tell you why that bothers me?" I half-heartedly lift my right hand to point to his hardhat.

"You can." It is an answer that sounds like, well, I *can* tell him, but it won't do any good. Perhaps I will be wasting my breath.

"It's just that you don't have any idea what it's like, you probably don't, and what I have to go through every day—"

He nods his head as though he is following this train of thought. "You mean at work."

"—Yes, at work of course, but not just here. Every moment, it's every moment just living my life, I have to think about this. I am always thinking about it. To think about the fact—that I'm not physically as big. That doesn't bother me much, but sometimes. And you don't know—"

At this point fat tears start leaking out, dropping out from under my safety glasses and skimming down my cheeks. "You don't know how many times I've been used because of that. That's all that's important. And how painful, how much damage that does to you emotionally—"

He takes off his safety glasses and I can see he is looking directly at me. The redness of his cheeks makes his gaze stand out. It is Tony. I take off my safety glasses.

I continue: "It does a lot of damage. And when I see something like that, it just tells me a lot about how you value women."

For a brief moment, he is quiet. Then, "I never looked at it that way." It could be a cliché line, but I don't think it is. He has never looked at it that way before. He continues: "I'm sorry." Tony has never looked at me like that before.

"You don't have to apologize; thank you for listening to me." I am flapping my arms around like a bird trying to take flight.

"I'll take the sticker off today. Actually, if you come back today, it will be gone before you come back, okay?"

I wipe my face, smile a little. "Okay, thanks for listening," I say, trying to move my feet, the other driver inching his truck forward in a hint for me to hurry up. I am caught between impulses, to continue thanking Tony, to shake his hand or something, to hurry back to the truck cab and get moving. I get moving.

I pull my truck out of the way, allowing the next driver to do his job. I spend a few minutes cleaning up the concrete from my chute. There's not much space at the jobsite, and I have to back all of the way out it, past the other truck, the pump, through the gate. As I move slowly backward past this scene, Tony looks at me, lifts his hard hat off his head, points. The sticker is gone.

•

Sometimes, they touch me.

I shriek. I jump when it happens.

Standing on your truck fender, so many feet off the ground, facing your chute and doing your job, busying yourself being a mixer driver, then a man comes up behind you, you don't see him, and he wants your attention—to say hi, to greet you, to be cute, to scare you, to ask for your water hose, to flirt—and grabs you by the ankles. Gives them a little squeeze.

Where do you see it written on my skin, this right to touch?

I've been standing on my truck, doing my job, and been ankle-grabbed by Bill, a driver from another plant. More than once.

I've been standing on my truck, doing my job, and been ankle-grabbed by Doug, a quality control guy from my company. I scream. He laughs.

I've been standing on my truck, doing my job waiting to pump concrete, and been ankle-grabbed by Mikey, my own Laforte Street driver. He thinks he's cute.

I've been standing on my truck, doing my job, and felt a light touch, a heavier touch, or a little shake, a little squeeze, and it's this guy or that one, smiling up at me.

I mentioned this once to Bob. "Kick 'em," he said. "Next time that happens, kick 'em in the face."

The next time it happens, it is dawn, and we are doing an early pour for Will's Concrete, a pump job for the university track. Again I am doing my work, standing on the truck looking at the chute and the concrete, watching the level in the pump hopper, my back necessarily turned toward anyone that approaches. I feel a hand close around each of my ankles. Startled, I shriek, and this time I do kick, not as hard as I can, but I punch my right leg out and back towards whoever it is that has his hands on my body.

I turn and look down. Will, the owner of the business, looks shocked. He stands there, eyes huge, stone still for a moment. He backs away from me and my truck. "What are you doing?" I yell. I glare. He is open-mouthed, hands outstretched for a moment more before they drop to his sides. "What makes you think you can just *touch* me?" I am almost snarling, no trace of my usual smile, only anger. I am embarrassed that once again, someone has made me scream in surprise, embarrassed that everyone turns and looks. Furious, hot, sick of it.

The work I am doing does not allow me to give any time to this, the pump sucking concrete without pity, and I turn my attention back to the job. Will and the men around him scatter; I don't bother to pay attention because any expectation of politeness from me has now been forfeited. I don't care.

I did not anticipate having to protect these parts of myself.

Never imagined rolling my jeans an inch at the bottom would leave the exposed skin vulnerable to touch. Never thought to be on guard about eyes and ankles that seemed so safe.

No body, no matter its shape, how it's dressed, its particular appeal, should have to worry about being touched. No body should have to protect itself from this. With a figure akin to the handle of a shovel, long and straight, I have been particularly immune to advances "because of" my body shape. Nothing to look at here.

So I got careless.

Careless, forgetting to think about what else was exposed. Careless, not maintaining constant vigilance lest someone approach. Careless, assuming that my body is my body, that nobody would dare to reach a hand out and touch it when I'm not looking, careless in assuming that it is safe at work.

Yet there is a little saving grace at the end of this story.

The next day, we do another early pour, again for Will's Concrete. I back my truck inside the big overhead door of the recycling center and climb down. I stand on the ground at the back, adding water to the load.

Will approaches. This time I see him. "Hey," he says, his voice a little worn and wrinkled like his face, where I also read concern about something. "I wanted to apologize for yesterday. I'm really sorry, I had no right to do that."

I look him in the eye, at the creases around his eyes, at something I see there and in the way his mouth turns down a little. I see written there that he understands what he has done, that there was no place for his touch. "I know I upset you and I'm sorry, I should have kept my hands to myself." He is still talking, and it is genuine.

I stand close to 138 with my hands wrapped around the parts of my truck and look at Will. I nod a little. "Thank you," I say, because it is all there is to say.

•

It is a long semester, but not a bad one. Yet fourteen weeks after it began, Spanish ends like no other class ever has for me. I speed-walk out of the classroom in tears, not bothering to say goodbye to Chuck or Lucia, whom I now feel friendly with, not wanting to say goodbye to the professor whom I had just decided was a complete ass. I hate him. I am also crushed, wanting approval, a word, just a single word, that I never get.

The final project had gone like most final projects go for me: I started strong, early in the semester, then put it off, thinking I had so much time, trying to win the little daily battles completing all the other things I had due, trying to keep an acceptable level of cleanliness in my house, trying to walk my Huskies occasionally.

Trying to haul concrete, trying to answer emails, trying not to give up and die a figurative but very dramatic death under a pile of student essays that never, ever, seemed to get smaller. Although my Spanish project text was approved months before, I might be forgiven for not having worked on the project until the final weeks. And this, the final weeks, was *early* for me. I knew there would be an added layer of complexity because the whole thing was in Spanish, so unlike those English papers, I hadn't waited until two or three days before to start. I didn't wait until the night before to write the bulk of it. I began early. I needed the time.

I was born disposed to put a ridiculous amount of pressure on myself. Or did I learn this somewhere? Wherever it came from, this "I have to be perfect" attitude has been something I have never rid myself of, although I try. I am rarely called out on it, which is why I feel relief when I am. In truck driving school, I struggled (or so I felt) to master the practice of alley docking. My irritation showed through the cracks in the middle of docking practice, and I remember, although this was now eighteen years ago, Brian the instructor standing there in the parking lot saying to me, "Linda, you don't have to be perfect." That diagnosis was so simple and so needed, a welcome intervention.

And yet the nauseating, relentless practice of having extremely high expectations for my level of ability in all things (except sports—there I am a realist) is securely in place come this final project for Spanish class. On top of that is the pressure of feeling like I must prove my place there, obviously being the student with the lowest level of language proficiency. And there is the pressure of wanting to please this professor, because when I submitted my project text, he showed genuine excitement. I want to do well, to justify that, to make him proud. Why, who knows. Even more importantly, there is the pressure of wanting to do well for Jaime, for Guatemala, for the literature of his country. It's funny to think about that, but Jaime has helped me so much with Spanish over the years, including proofreading homework for this class, it feels like he's a part of it. I toss pressure upon pressure on top of the pile.

The text is the nineteenth-century Guatemalan writer José Batres Montúfar's *Poesias*, which contains a selection of his poetry, including the three long verses collectively known as "Tradiciones de Guatemala." These long poems are what Montúfar is famous for, or as famous as a nineteenth-century poet from Guatemala could be in the self-centered mainstream culture of twenty-first-century United States. I choose it because it is Guatemalan, it fits the time period required, and there is little written about it. The professor, as he flips through *Poesias* when I bring it to him for approval, is smiling, animated, the pitch of his voice just a little higher. I feel confident, like the material is there.

Confident, that is, until I open *Poesias* to begin my work. Suddenly I remember that I am not a poet, and that poetry is not the same as prose, and that poetry in a language I am still fighting to learn is not poetry in a language I already know well. It is not long before I break into a sweaty panic. What will I write about? What clever, no, *brilliant* paper can I conjure?

It is an April Saturday and beginning to get nice outside in Lincoln, beautiful weather that I can't enjoy adding another layer of frustration to my work. Instead, I sit on my couch, inside the little house where I have spent the whole winter cooped up, up to my armpits in semi-relevant sources about Montúfar that aren't helping me a bit. It is Jaime's custom to stop over after he is done working on Saturdays, and this day is no different.

He arrives midday and I complain about my woes. "I'll help you," he says in Spanish. "We can look at it together; I'll help you before I leave." So before he leaves my house that day, we take a piece of chocolate cake that I have baked, a tiny can of Sprite, my laptop, and Montúfar's *Poesias* to my front porch and sit on the stoop. As Jaime shovels cake in, I show him the poem I think has the most potential. The poem is "Al Volcan de Agua," and is only a few pages, for me a manageable length.

"But what do you have to write?" Jaime asks me. I explain the concept of the academic paper: "I need to find one or two poems here, and to say something about them that no one has said before. I need to read the poems, and then try to come up with an idea, why they are important."

This is one of my favorite memories with Jaime. As he had sat down on the stoop with a plate of cake in his hand, he looked around my yard, up and down the street with the trees in bloom, and said in English, "Wow, nice," drawing out the "wow" and emphasizing the first part of "nice" like he does. As we sit side-by-side on the concrete step, dissecting "Al Volcan de Agua," we have *fun*. We read the poem together, line by line, and translate. I type notes of the comments he makes. We look up words together that neither of us know, and when he leaves, I feel animated and confident. He is excited about a poem. His excitement makes me excited. I can do this.

And I do. The final paper is a little messy, a little disconnected from one idea to the other. I struggle. But I am also happy with the experience of the project and feel like it is something I can continue to work on after the semester ends. There is so little work done on Montúfar, and it could be something special to publish an article about his poetry, to contribute: I, who holds such great contempt for writing the academic article. My introduction and conclusion are personal, as I think they should be: after all, what good is a paper if you can't do something with it outside the classroom?

In this Spanish class, in addition to writing this eighteen- to twenty-page paper, we are asked to present it as if we were in a symposium. The instructor requests that we have a one-page handout with key points and a visual presentation. So I do all of this, making a snappy handout, quite concise, and a clean, crisp, engaging PowerPoint. The other students do one or the other.

Chuck reads his paper out loud almost word for word, and the professor makes some comments at the end: "Very interesting, the idea of . . . ." We take a short break, and Lucia is the only one to leave the room. As we wait for her to return, Chuck gets more feedback from the professor: "It's difficult to find anything new to say about a text that's been written about so much." Chuck is a language major, not a literature major, and the professor seems zoned in on the potential for these papers to be read at an actual symposium. Chuck politely nods and responds little.

Next up is Lucia, the clear favorite of the professor: I have little idea what she is talking about (my fault, not hers), but her presentation is lively and she seems very knowledgeable. The professor eats it up, eagerly asking several questions at the end. This is great for Lucia, who is sharp, studious, and kind, and I only hope for a "Thanks, that's interesting," after I make my own presentation.

I make my way to the front of the room and ready my paper and my PowerPoint. The professor sits immediately in front of the podium where I stand. The paper is too long to share in its entirety, so I choose to read most of my introductory comments and make selections from the rest of my text, as instructed. My introductory comments amount to little more than a page, and they are important to frame the project:

*In the process of sorting through the work by nineteenth-century Guatemalan poet José Batres Montúfar, I became stressed. I read poem after poem, searching for just the right thing to write about in this particular moment. A lyric poem titled "Al Volcan de Agua" caught my attention, and I read it. I liked it. A close friend from Guatemala, who has no college experience, volunteered to read it again with me to help with my translation. He saw my stress and wanted to help. After we had gone through the poem together, we sat for a moment in silence. "Entonces?" I said. "Que?" he replied. "There is nothing to write about!" In my mounting frustration to say just the right thing, my eternal academic struggle for brilliance, my need to impress, I panicked. But my friend was calm. "But what do you mean?" he asked. "There is so much here!"*

*In that moment, he was excited. In that moment, his excitement calmed me down. In retrospect, it also humbled me. His comment was a gift. This man who had never read a poem before, found so much in a short lyric by Montúfar when I could see nothing. I was making things too difficult. I needed to slow down and enjoy the poem. After all, there is so much here.*

I greatly underestimate how hard it will be to read aloud in academic Spanish for twenty minutes: my throat is dry, I am shaking, and I verbally stumble over and over. Lucia nods encouragingly. Chuck is attentive and polite. Only a few feet away, I cannot look directly at the professor as he keeps shifting in his seat, taking his glasses on and off. My sense tells me he is not happy.

But what I really am not prepared for is his silence. He says absolutely nothing at all at the end of my presentation.

Nothing at all.

Well—let me correct that. For pure joy, I put a picture of Guatemala's national bird, the resplendent quetzal, on my final slide. It is a beautiful creature, and important to the country, a symbol on books, currency, food packaging, and more. I think people will enjoy seeing it. As I stand there at the front of the room in postpresentation silence, the professor looks at the slide and says with a smirk on his face, "I think I killed one of those when I was younger."

And that is it.

There is no "Gracias Linda." No "Buen trabajo." No "Interesante." Certainly no questions or comments. I stand at the podium for an extra few seconds, waiting. Surely there will be something besides the quetzal comment. There is not. There is nothing. Nothing. I return to my seat.

The rest of the class, which is mercifully short, is painful. Grateful to have a mask on so they can't see the crumpling of my face, I alternate my gaze between the front of the room and the professor as he makes his final comments to the class. I can't look at Lucia or Chuck, and hope no one notices as I try to nonchalantly wipe away the tears that are starting to come. Nothing? As soon as he releases us, I jump out of the seat, push my notebook and folder into my backpack, and rush out of the room into the hall before a sob gives it all away.

Lucia, who normally packs up slowly, is right behind me, Chuck on her heels. She leaves her things at her desk as they rush out to catch me before I leave, giving me words of encouragement I don't expect, but am grateful for. As we stand together in the foyer of the stairwell, the professor walks out of the classroom, not glancing our way, not a word to us, and makes his exit down the opposite end of the hall.

His final paper comments? About my opening pages, the professor writes: "Páginas 1 y 2 estan fuera de lugar para un trabajo formal. Una nota aparte sería mejor."

There was no place in a formal work for my opening story. A separate note, he writes, would be better.

Unequivocally, the professor wants me to tell the same story we already know. Follow the template. The tradition. The standard, the expected. There is no room for my tale of struggle with the poem, or of witnessing Jaime finding joy within it. Our real, felt experiences are not part of this academic narrative, like "finishando" is, no doubt, not part of the Spanish language.

•

When I try to engage my students in the second chapter from Paulo Freire's *Pedagogy of the Oppressed*, which is the chapter about our deeply flawed system of education, they are often puzzled by one the of the opening lines: "Education is suffering from narration sickness." "What does he mean?" they ask me. I tell them that I interpret this to mean that teachers narrate, or talk and talk, trying to deposit, without reflection, the "right" knowledge into the minds of students, without wanting any interaction from those students. This is a teacher, I explain, that enjoys just lecturing you. This is a teacher that doesn't want anyone to ask questions or who invites only the "right" questions. Freire explains:

> The banking approach to adult education, for example, will never propose to students that they critically consider reality. It will deal instead with such vital questions as whether Roger gave green grass to the goat, and insist upon the importance of learning that, on the contrary, Roger gave green grass to the rabbit. The 'humanism' of the banking approach masks the effort to turn women and men into automatons—the very negation of their ontological vocation to be more fully human.

I give my students this chapter at the beginning of each semester, asking them to think about their stake in their education and inviting them to participate as teachers, as well as inviting them to consider me as a fellow student. Regardless of how well the discussion surrounding Freire's work goes, the idea of teachers sharing responsibilities with students and vice versa remains difficult to adapt to. I aspire to it, I welcome my students to it, but we have been brainwashed well over a lifetime. Yet realizing that banking education cannot be undone in a semester does not mean that we can't, as "teachers," go a long way to provide students the freedom to express ways of thinking that might be new to us, to explore connections that might never occur to us, to allow a divergence from the system in the interests of supporting a student in *their real interests.*

This is not without risks. An educator who has invested a lifetime in curating their education risks an exposure to what they do not know and worse, they risk finding out there is much *they do not know*; an educator who reaps the daily rewards of a strutting authority at the front of a classroom risks an unraveling of that authority. Yet there are greater risks: a professor's insistence on narrow academic rules risks damaging a student committed to exploring the world around her. An insistence on academia in isolation, maintains a split between "us" inside and those on the outside. These are great risks.

It's almost funny to think about the fear that keeps an educator from allowing real people and the real world into an academic article, into their classroom, funny that this would *bother* someone so. Simultaneously it is not funny at all since the institutions and systems that form this mode of thinking (this banking mode) have a tangible effect on oppressed people's ability to survive and thrive.

While I want to make clear the seriousness of this, the problem it causes for real people in our world, I also choose here to laugh a little: so you see, you've not done me damage, profesor, you've simply given me the opportunity to raise my consciousness even more.

# Mouse

In the batch office, Darren says to everyone, smiling as he throws a fist in the air (apropos but unsolicited as if to contextualize one woman's presence among men):

"We're all talking and then you hear a little voice like 'Yeah!' and it's Linda."

# Lacking

The university is not the only place where there are certain . . . expectations.

When I reply that I don't have kids, the concrete guys say, "Really?!" or better still, "That's okay, there's still time," as if to console me, as if I am worried.

So I say, "No, I don't want kids, not now, not ever," and I get looks like I'm one very strange woman. Am I even a woman at all? I am not a mother and don't want to be. Ever. This is hard for people to understand.

So I gesture toward my mixer truck and say, "Where would I put a baby in here? There's not even a passenger seat." They laugh, even though I was not joking. I hope I've made my point. My point is that I drive because I love to drive, for the thrill and the skill of it. And that's enough.

I love to drive. It is a privilege to choose the work I do. I could look for something else; something with less hours, less wear and tear on my body, something, especially now that I have my doctorate, with better pay. But I keep driving, because of all the jobs out there, driving seems like the thing I was made to do.

It's acceptable, understandable, for a woman to work for others, especially for children. Because women are mothers and that's what mothers do. They give, selflessly, and to be selfless is good, for women. Perhaps this is why my answer about "no kids" unsettles people; it reveals me, reveals that I am working for myself. I am working because I have to. I am working for the love of the work. I am working and saving, working and planning, working and working for myself.

I've searched for other texts that show women like me. They are very hard to find.

In 2021, Amy Butcher published *MotherTrucker: Finding Joy on the Loneliest Road in America*. It's a story about Joy Weibe, truck driver. I thought this might be it, something to latch on to, someone to identify with. But the book wasn't what I expected.

In *MotherTrucker*, Butcher, a thirty-something professor who lives and works in Ohio, travels to Fairbanks to meet Weibe, fifty, after becoming enamored with her story via Instagram. As Butcher's own story unravels along with Weibe's, readers learn the motivation for her trip. Trapped inside an abusive relationship, Butcher is drawn to Weibe as an escape and someone to learn from. Butcher's trip to Fairbanks is a pilgrimage that might spur a resolution to the pain she admits to living in within her own home and relationship.

Joy Weibe is an "ice road trucker," like Lisa Kelly. Butcher's writing about Weibe is a chance to know a female truck driver without the gloss and manipulative drama the History Channel producers inevitably layered over *Ice Road Truckers* (*IRT*), which "documented" truck drivers travelling up and down what is dubbed America's most dangerous road, Alaska's Dalton Highway. The Dalton stretches from Fairbanks to Prudhoe Bay, an oilfield settlement as far north as one can go via road. The road is almost four hundred miles long and has practically no services. Snow, mountain passes, unpaved roads, ice, blizzards and whiteouts, wildlife, and avalanches are just some of the hazards that make the Dalton a dangerous place to work. Weibe is one of the ice road truckers that drives the Dalton day in and day out. Importantly though, and the book makes this distinction clear: she is one of the people who risk their lives to do this job *each day, without* the glamour of a cable network documenting, and likely scripting, their moves. Butcher is sure to note claims from Weibe's coworkers that call her the *only* female ice road trucker on the Dalton, notwithstanding the three women who appeared on *IRT*.

 I came to *MotherTrucker* hoping to read about work, hoping for someone to write about trucking. I wanted to read a book from a woman who loved machines and driving and doing the work those things entailed. I wanted to learn more about the Ice Road, what it was like to drive it, what it was like for another woman to do this job among men. I wanted all those details. I wanted to read, finally, about a perspective that might match my own, or maybe about one that differed from it. At least I would have something to compare my own experiences against, something that would come close to me.

 I was disappointed. Not in the book, exactly, but in the failure to find what I've been searching for. It's lonely. Weibe and Butcher do make a trip up and down the Dalton, but because of an ill-timed knee injury, they make the trek in Weibe's pickup and not her semi-truck. This necessarily keeps the reader at a distance from the many nuances of Weibe's daily drive, from the felt sense of the truck. Consequently, we are compelled to focus instead on the journey the women make in the pickup, although it's still one that offers a glimpse into life on the Dalton. As Butcher accompanies Weibe up the Ice Road and interacts with the drivers, waitresses, hotel staff, and oilfield workers they meet along the way, readers learn what draws these men and women to their work, about their humanity despite the stereotypes they are often labeled with, and about the loneliness the work invites. And the book is, after all, about the Dalton Highway. Weibe consistently draws Butcher's attention to the landscape and to the native people and animals who inhabit the lands the Dalton bisects. Readers are invited to understand the beauty and power of this road along with its danger, and the impacts it has on the living world, for better, maybe, and for worse.

But we never really learn about that woman and her truck.

The trip gives Weibe and Butcher time to share their stories, including Weibe's motivations for driving and the consequences her job has on her spirituality and family life. And although the gravity of things isn't revealed until the end, throughout the text there are clues that Weibe herself, like Butcher, has a history of abusive relationships in her life—a history she is certainly not safe and clear from, even up until that moment.

The book's subtitle comes much closer to explaining what the book is about: "finding joy on the loneliest road in America." Butcher literally finds Joy Weibe on the Dalton. Joy drives the Dalton to provide financial security for herself and her teenage daughter, but she also finds joy, in the form of her belief in god, in the people and the landscape of northern Alaska. And then there's Butcher, who finds in herself the force she needs to return to Ohio and change the world she's been living in, discovering her strength. As the narrative of the trip unfolds, so does the narrative of Butcher's life with her abusive partner, so much so that this narrative takes over the text and becomes the focal point and lens in which we experience Weibe's life. *MotherTrucker* reaches a horrible end when, only four months after Butcher's visit, Weibe unexpectedly dies on the Dalton. Fellow drivers find her and her tanker-trailer, rolled over an embankment that Weibe simply hadn't been able to see in a storm.

*MotherTrucker* would have been a different book if Weibe had lived. Butcher had planned a return visit; Weibe's death happened only a few weeks before. It was an unexpected and personal loss for Butcher as well as for Weibe's children and countless friends. We'll never know the rest of that story.

I do not want to belittle the story that was told—not for one second—but I long for a story told by a woman about herself, about her work with machines, about the adventure of it. One where partners and children do not interrupt the narrative and become a focal point, where they are not the motivation, the thing to run to or away from. I want a story that is work for work's sake. It feels blasphemous to even type such a thing.

The title for Butcher's text says a lot. The moniker "Mother Trucker" was born when Weibe was brainstorming an Instagram handle, and her adult son suggested this play on the pervasive profanity. Obviously Weibe was a badass truck driver; she did a dangerous job and did it well, was respected by everyone around her. Her role as a mother was also a critical part of who she was: it was *the* reason she worked on the Dalton: to provide for and give future security to her daughter. Both parts of her identity blended to become the book's title, but notice, "trucker" is joined to "mother." Inseparable.

There's another recent nonfiction text about work, and this one written by the person who experienced it. In 2019 Stephanie Land published *Maid: Hard Work, Low Pay, and a Mother's Will to Survive*, later made into a Netflix series. *Maid*, as you might guess, is about survival, about what it takes (and it takes a lot) to clean up after other people for a wage, an exceptionally detailed account of one of the most thankless types of work.

But again in *Maid*, working women are working to support families. Like Weibe in *MotherTrucker*, providing for her daughter is Land's motivation to keep going; at times it is the only thing that keeps her moving in an exhausting fight through poverty. Like *MotherTrucker*, we know instantly that motherhood is key since we see it in the subtitle. I realize that the way the book was named might not have been Land's choice (although it might have been); it is entirely possible that the publisher figured "motherhood" would draw buyers. A lone woman is one thing (dangerous, untouchable, perhaps tainted), but a woman on a fight to save her daughter—that's entirely another. And yet, the text really *is* about Land's incredible stamina and fight to make sure her daughter could be cared for, despite finding herself in a situation where earning a livable wage was almost impossible. *Maid* does a better job than *MotherTrucker* of getting close to the work, but Land authored her own story, and Weibe relied on Butcher to tell hers. Again and again, Land tells us what it is like to clean houses for a living, the repetition of her stories reinforcing the frustration of the struggles and indignities that accompany the working poor.

There is joy in *Maid* too, and that joy rests entirely in Land's daughter Mia.

I don't criticize Butcher, Land, or Weibe; I write this out of frustration that women's experiences are expected to center on family. Motherhood displaces almost everything else. I understand that for some mothers, motherhood actually does displace almost everything else, but I reject the assumption that women can, or should, *automatically* relate to this. Motherhood is not intrinsic in all women. This seemingly radical choice, given the culture I am surrounded by, is alienating. Contemporary texts about labor become distant. Were they published because they are exemplars of women giving, always giving for others? What about women working for their own sake, for the love or the necessity of the work, without a family attached?

# Talking Back

He tells me they are going to need a little more concrete right there, and I shake my head no and smile. "Are you sure?" I ask. "I think you have it!"

I have never poured for this group before, never even heard of them, but they've been joking lightly with me since the beginning, so things feel easy, chill, good.

Yet I say, "I think you have it!" and he looks up at me, glances over at his compañero, then back at me. "You sure do like to talk back," he says.

•

It is 100 degrees outside, and Nebraska's strangling humidity layers over searing heat. A dozen Latino men mill about, sit in the shade, wait next to their tools. The sun is fierce and the breeze is slight. I can't imagine how much hotter it is within the stifled, confined space of the truck drum. This pour is going to be a rough one.

I stand on my fender and bring the concrete up, letting it fall from the drum a little so Jesus can tell me if he wants water added. A heavy white man stands next to him, younger than Jesus; they are both wearing gray TLC Construction hats, gray TLC Construction T-shirts. The white guy looks up at the concrete and proclaims, "It looks good to me." The concrete is very stiff, very stiff, so stiff.

I look at this man I don't know and hear myself saying, without smiling, "Well you're not the one holding the shovel." He looks at me with surprise before turning his attention back to Jesus.

"How much you have?" Jesus asks me. He wants to know how many yards of concrete I brought.

"Nueve," I answer, as the other man answers "nine" simultaneously.

"Nueve," Jesus says to himself. He puts his palm up and folds in his thumb, leaving four fingers in the air. "Add four gallons please."

The white guy looks at Jesus, who is already moving again, ready to pour. "I don't want to hear you whine when it doesn't stick," he says.

•

"When listeners hear a female voice," writes Mary Beard, "they do not hear a voice that connotes authority; or rather they have not learned how to hear authority in it." The voice itself, its tone and cadence, the words it speaks, the body it flows from, all of these flag a subconscious warning to the male listener (is listener too generous a word?): there are limitations to her knowledge. Can we even call it knowledge?

When a person reframes a woman's expertise as "talking back," talks down to someone with lesser authority, or acts like they don't hear me speaking (but definitely do hear me speaking), all cut me and believe me, I do bleed. They are tactics not so different from what certain professors use in classrooms, clinging to their own traditions at the expense of their students' hearts and minds. Powerful weapons. Moments that hurt. Not being taken seriously or being ignored *hurts*. I can feel it even as I write this.

I don't like to be silenced in the classroom, but it's exponentially more painful when I'm driving my truck, working. Why, I wonder. Perhaps it feels more personal. Beard shows us, from the public speech of Roman times through political speech today, how women were and are allowed to speak for women (sometimes), on our own behalf, but how the game changes when we dare to speak for the community at large. Surrounded by men in construction, I am tolerated, perhaps even welcomed as an anomaly, when I smile, am pleasant, do my job well. When I make no waves, when I ask no questions. But when I say, "Hey, I think you've got enough there" or "Hey, I think you do need to add a little water," well, what changes?

I level the playing field. I can do this too. I've infiltrated. I've made it through.

This is when their guard goes up and the guns come out. Does it help knowing that the moments I'm belittled are nothing more than someone feeling threatened, feeling afraid, feeling like they must *defend* a suddenly precarious position? Sometimes, yeah. Sometimes I see how pathetic their behavior is and I pity them (just a little) as I stand there wrapped in the power I've claimed for myself. Sometimes it empowers me to push back, not just hanging on but expanding my territory, expanding our territory. Sometimes the perspective I've gained helps, lets me live another day as strong as ever.

But sometimes it doesn't help one bit. I falter and I wonder and I feel like someone's sliced open my chest as I stand there and watch my hurt and fear of worthlessness gush out of me in agonizing bloody slowness.

That's okay. To a point. I'm human.

As long as I get up again, keep moving. And loudly.

# Blindside

Some people I trusted, put my confidence in, until they exposed their true selves. Taught me more about the world, made me sadder, made me tougher.

When it came to the job, Dan was one of the pump operators that I had total confidence in. The way he carried himself, personality, vibe, whatever you wanted to call it, you could whittle it down to that he just seemed to know what he was doing. He moved slowly, deliberately, sometimes laboriously. And although I doubt that he was more than ten years older than me, Dan had a paternal aura about him. Maybe because he wore suspenders and had salt and pepper hair. Maybe because he called me "dear" in a fatherly way that didn't feel degrading. I had total confidence in how Dan could do his job. Like all the pump operators I knew (save one, but he was a nightmare to everyone) Dan treated me well, no different than anyone else.

Until the day, as the story always goes, that he didn't. Not far from Laforte Street, tucked between an old sprawling cemetery and an old humble neighborhood, we were pouring footings for what looked to be new townhouses. The customer, Zabka Concrete, had ordered more than one hundred yards. It was a busy spring day, and I'd end up hauling three loads here, back-to-back.

Dan was the pump operator. The first load went off without a hitch; I remember laughing with him over some joke about Midnight, over the anticipated wait on trucks to arrive, something like that. Over the prior three summers I'd become confident, efficient, really good at what I was doing. For that first load I arrived, did the job, quickly packed up and left, knowing I'd likely be returning, not wanting to keep the guys waiting on their concrete.

I did return, quickly, with a second load. Like the first, it was dry, and I stood at the back on the platform of the truck, ready to add water. I wish I could tell you, reader, what comment sparked what happened next, but I can no longer remember. Was it chatter about plans for the weekend? Boredom? My mind won't go back and reach it.

And that's probably because I am still awed, in a terrible sort of way, remembering what Dan said to me, the thing that I can't forget or block out. As I stood on the back of my truck, adding water to the load, doing my job, Dan, the same Dan I've worked with for years and never had even a glimmer of trouble with says, "At least you've got a pair of titties to play with."

I laughed. I laughed because that could not possibly have been what this man said, and I was sure that he had actually said, "At least you've got a pair of kitties to play with." You know, kitties, cats, pets. My two dogs, my mind reasoned—he must've mistakenly thought I had cats.

But how did he know I had dogs? Had I mentioned the huskies before?

"What's that?" I laughed, having difficulty hearing over the roar of my truck drum spinning fast, mixing in the water, the anticipatory hum of the pump truck, waiting on me. How did he know I had dogs? Was that what he said?

"At least you have a pair of titties to play with." Dan stood on the ground next to the pump, controls slung around his neck, looking up and waiting on me.

A pair of kitties? Oh, I reasoned, he must have said a pair of kiddies.

But I don't have children. Why would he think I had children?

"What did you say?" I leaned forward slightly to hear better, my smile gone now in the confusion, and asked again.

"At least you have a pair of titties to play with," Dan told me, as unabashedly as he had twice prior. "You know, I read in a magazine somewhere that that's why women are happier than men."

And then, only then, did I get it. At least I had a pair of titties to play with. Of course that was what he said, of course it was.

I stood on 138. Looked down at Dan. He looked at me, unphased. "I don't find that funny," I said, straight-faced.

"You don't?" from Dan. "Luckily it doesn't bother me what anyone else thinks."

I stared open-mouthed after him as he walked away. Flushed. Dumbfounded. But the job wouldn't wait for me to process anything. The pump kicked on, sucking concrete, and I pushed the controls for my drum and poured, did what I needed to do, left. Drove back to Laforte Street with tunnel vision, still not processing, just in disbelief.

And of course, I get there and there's no one else at the plant, so I'm immediately loaded with my third load to the same job. Headed back. When I arrived back at the jobsite, I put my dark safety glasses on to cover my eyes. I backed up to the pump and climbed out the cab. Head down, eyes on my boots and the dirt, I walked to the back of the truck where Dan was waiting.

His attitude had changed. "Hey," he said, no smile on his face this time. His tone had changed. I barely lifted my head from the ground where I was still focused, cocking it just enough to look at him sideways as I climbed up on 138.

"Hey," he said, "I'm really sorry if I offended you. That was not my intention. I'm sorry."

Still barely looking at him, expressionless, I gave a single nod, then folded back into myself. He marched away, purposefully, fleeing the scene of his apology. I poured the load and left without saying a word to anyone, also fleeing.

But back at the plant, as the last truck was loaded and I knew I didn't have to return again, that was another story. Still in disbelief, I wanted to tell someone. I didn't want to, didn't know how to, but I wanted someone to hear me. I wanted, in hindsight, someone to experience it with me.

Sebas was the first driver I saw, and also a work friend. Sebas put on a sort of lovably naive attitude most of the time, but he was deeper than that. Sebas would do. I caught up to him as we were both coming in the door of the building. He smiled his big goofy grin, head tilted back, cheap yellow-rimmed sunglasses on his face. I had an almost identical pair, salmon colored. Sebas had given them to me after I admired them. We both liked bright colors.

"Hey," I said, "Look, can I tell you what just happened to me?"

"What?" He grinned and pushed his glasses onto his head. "Telllll me."

Flushed, I had to heave the words out, drawing them up and out of my chest and throat, whispering and embarrassed. We were standing inside the doorway now, and Sebas's eyes grew big.

"I mean, when would you ever say something like that?"

"Not me," Sebas's head flew back and forth for emphasis. "I would never say that." The look on his face told me he wouldn't. "Wow."

And that tiny release of pressure was enough. I wasn't going to say anything more about it. I hadn't even considered that an option. But I was angry, twisted and upset. I arrived home from work several hours later, let the dogs out, fell onto the couch and sat there staring at nothing. And cried a little. I had plenty I wanted to do around the house that evening, but I couldn't move from the couch. I sat there and stared out the window, at the wall.

When Jaime called later, as usual, I knew I would tell him, and it would end with that. For me, things that might be emotionally hard to say in English are easier in Spanish, lacking lifelong intimacy with its words. But this was just as almost impossible to say in Spanish.

Jaime was not pleased. He listened in silence for a moment as I snuffed and sniffled and stifled more crying. There on my couch, in my own home, I felt weaker trying to utter something that now seemed more invasive. I had been fighting the urge all afternoon to wrap my arms around myself, to cross them, to cover up. In Spanish, Jaime was adamant. "You have to tell Midnight, guapa. Midnight should support you. The pump truck is a business that works with Midnight, and this isn't okay. If they don't support you, you call somebody else."

I sat, drooping, and listened. I said okay to appease him as Jaime's anger with the pump truck operator gained traction. I assured him, halfheartedly, I'd talk to someone the next day. I'm not sure why. I felt tiny, like I didn't even have half a heart.

I didn't want to talk to anyone else, didn't see the point. Although I promised Jaime I would, I wasn't sure I'd follow through. The problem was that the businesses that owned these pump trucks and employed the operators weren't our customers: our customers were also their customers. So in this instance,

Zabka, buying the concrete, was Midnight's customer. Zabka had hired Midwest Pumping to pump it. Midnight really had nothing to do with Midwest.

Which is why this wasn't the same situation as T&T. Because the pump operator was a middleman, hired by and contacted by our customers, we never knew who would be where. It would have been impossible for Midnight to promise me that I'd never go to a job where Dan was, because they barely knew what jobs would be pumped, let alone what company would be pumping and which of their operators would be there. And frankly, I was not one for throwing that flag anyway. My "don't send me back" mandate was different with T&T, since there was an ever-present visual reminder with them of the misogyny they promoted: I'd literally have it in my face whenever I poured. People staying stupid shit was different. I had no desire for my employer to have a long list of places where I couldn't go. Running wasn't how I wanted to deal with problems. I suppose my way of dealing was just to bury them.

But I followed through the next day. I had promised Jaime, and it seemed the least I could do. I would make the formal gesture. And I realized that by sharing with the managers at Laforte Street, I might expose them to what it was like for a woman working around men. This was motivation. Maybe they would understand our perspectives just a tiny bit more. Maybe it would help. Lenny, the plant superintendent, wasn't around though, so in the afternoon I sat in my mixer and labored over a text message:

Hi, are you going to be around later this week or perhaps the beginning of next? I was wondering if I might chat a little with you, Howard, and Chip? Nothing to worry about: it's not a I'm quitting/I'm angry/etc. talk. It's just that someone at the job yesterday said another gross and thoughtless thing to me, and rather than just bury it and internalize it, literally the least I can do to try and make something better from that moment would be to share it with others, as awkward as that will be for all of us. Please think about it and let me know if you have a little time, thank you!

His reply came four minutes later.

I'll be in tomorrow, but I'd rather not wait until then. Should I have the GM call you?

Wow no, the last thing I was going to do was repeat this to someone from the office, crisp and clean and corporate. I'd probably die first.

We agreed to meet tomorrow.

How did it happen that I found myself the next afternoon sitting in Howard's office next to Chip, Howard behind his desk, Lenny perched in a chair by the window with a yellow pad and a pen ready in his hands? I sat there and smiled nervously, despite being comfortable with all of them, gripping the handles of the chair and fighting the compulsion to cross my arms over my chest.

"So," Lenny said, "What happened?" Before I explained anything about it, I wanted to let them know why I had asked to see them, why I thought this was worth the trouble. That I knew sometimes they were curious about how I was treated on jobs. That to sit and suffer over a comment was at least worth something if I tried to make something out of it. I then launched into the details: me arriving at the job, making small talk, everything fine, coming back for the second—

"I want to know what this guy said." Lenny wasn't being rude to me, but almost tipping out of his chair with anger, or anxiety, or something.

I felt my face flush. I looked down. I pulled at the hem of my shirt and looked around at everyone. "I'm sorry, it's just hard to repeat," I said. I grinned a deranged grin and kept looking at the floor, the three small plants lined up neatly on the sill, at my boots, the corner of the desk. "I thought about writing it down but decided that would be even weirder."

The guys laughed sympathetically.

"Well. Well, he said, umm, he said that, uh, if I ever get bored . . . that . . . that . . ." I lowered my voice and looked at my lap. "That at least I have a pair of titties to play with."

Lenny had been taking notes as I pushed the sentence out, but at my mention of my body he stopped short and looked up at me. Silent, mouth open, he looked down again and wrote. Chip's hand flew up to his forehead and he covered his eyes, dragging his hand down across his face.

Howard leaned back in his chair and gazed around the room.

"Who said this?" Lenny asked. He stared at me.

I looked at him. "It was Dan."

He cursed and beat the pen against the notepad, looking at Howard. "And he's Midwest's right-hand man!," they talked between themselves. "He's been practically running that place since they've sold it."

I watched, still, from my chair near the door. It sounded like they knew Dan, knew the pump operators, which surprised me. I hadn't imagined that guys in the plant, office people, would know the people I knew out there. I hadn't expected any overlap between this place and that one.

Chip was silent. New to Midnight, he didn't know Dan, didn't know any of them. Howard rocked in his desk chair. I crossed my arms, my ankles, uncrossed them.

They tried to unpack it:

"What kind of comment is that, anyway?"

"Yeah, who says that?"

"I mean, why would you—why would you bring that up? Where'd that come from?"

"Dan should know better."

Lenny looked at me. "Linda, I'm sorry."

"Oh, it's not your fault," I said, pulling at my shirt hem and sitting a little more upright in the chair. "It's just, maybe it doesn't seem like a big thing." Elbows on the armrests now, I laced my fingers together, leaning forward and into myself. "But I wish people would understand how to respect a woman's body."

Silent. I thought.

Silent.

"You've taught me so much over the years." Lenny said it quietly. I tilted my head and brought my eyes up. He was looking at me, then ahead of him, into a space I couldn't see. Time slipped back infinitely fast to my first day there, when he was still the Laforte Street supervisor.

Younger days. Time raced forward. I couldn't grasp any of it, but it was all there. I had never imagined. He brought his eyes up to meet mine, still holding pen and notepad, and I stared.

He inhaled and let it out, and the room snapped back. "Linda, I want you to know that I need to take this to my boss, and HR." Chip blew out a firm "yes" of relief, Howard murmured assent. I started.

"That's not why I'm here. I just wanted you to know."

Howard and Lenny exchanged nods and looks. "There are other women that work for Midnight, other women out there. You don't want this guy saying this to someone else. We have a lot of other plants, and Midwest pumps all over, in Omaha, in Iowa."

My mind jumped to Katelyn, to Josephine, to women still unnamed, shadow figures of the future, out there working. For the first time, I thought of other women. "I didn't think of that." I hadn't. I replayed it in my mind with Kate standing on a truck. Josie. Saw their faces. If I could take that moment from them, for them.

I sat up, taller. "No, I hadn't thought of that." The vacuum began to fade from around me. Women drivers in Omaha, how many? Beatrice? How many? I wasn't the only one. I nodded. "I understand." But what would happen. "But what will happen?" I asked. I still had to work with Dan.

"I'm not sure," Lenny said. "I'll talk to Heather across the street."

Unsure of what to say, I sat there, thinking, looking at each one of them, the door still closed behind us, the world beyond it still moving, my guys still loading and hauling loads, meeting the customers, relationships unfolding every moment. Lenny was a company man, someone who was here first for the mission of supplying an exceptional product, of excelling in the name of Midnight Concrete Company. Our angles of vision intersected, but neither originated nor ended in the same point.

"As a manager, it's my responsibility to follow up on this," he said, tapping the yellow pad twice with that pen. I nodded and said nothing to the contrary.

"Thanks for listening to me, thanks for your time," I said. Everyone nodded. Howard made a joke and smiled, we all laughed. I was anxious to go back to my truck and I wasn't; dejected and still surprised that I was having this conversation at work, but somehow content, because we were having conversation, about women's bodies but not in the usual way, at work.

The following week I receive a call from Peter, the general manager of Midnight. He has Heather from human resources on the line. The call catches me off guard and I'm not sure what to say, not sure what they want to know. At first I think they are concerned for me; perhaps they are (I wonder, now, what Heather thought when she heard of the incident, how the conversation would have been different if it was only her on the line). Then I understand that this call is a move they must make, a formal acknowledgment of a complaint. "We've sent a letter to Midwest," Peter tells me. I wonder, but don't interrupt to ask, if he means an actual, paper letter. I picture someone printing this out, wonder who it was, see the words on the page and cringe thinking someone had to type them, imagine the type of paper one uses for formal letters these days, picture someone folding it, licking an envelope. As the conversation closes Peter thanks me, apologizes again, and says they won't keep me any longer, they imagine I have work to do.

And it's true. My truck number will be up any moment. The entirety of our talk took place while I was working, me never still during a moment of it, not having been given the chance.

A final scene. A week and a half later I get a text message from Peter, asking me to call him when I can. I am about to leave for a job but resolve to call him when I'm done pouring, before I arrive back at plant and get sucked into the system, available to be sent out again at moment's notice.

I finish the pour at a new parking garage downtown. It was an easy one, no chutes to clean, and I am under the O Street viaduct in a parking lot. It's shady, and I can make a phone call without worrying I am in someone's way. I pick up the phone and hit Peter's desk number.

He answers on the second ring and is friendly, moving the conversation forward so I don't have to. He begins by explaining again that a letter was sent to Midwest—

"A real letter?" I interrupt. "Like a paper one?"

"Yes, a real letter," he says. "And we received one in reply." He went on to explain that Midwest had told Midnight they would follow up with Dan in one of two ways, which was up to Midnight. "So it's up to us, it's up to you, Linda, what you'd like to do. The choice is entirely yours."

"Option one," he continues, "Is to send Dan to training to educate him on this behavior. Once he's completed the training, Midwest will send Midnight proof of its completion."

"Okay," I say, nodding to myself in the cab. Seems standard and reasonable. What then, could option two be?

"Option two," Peter explains, "Is that they'll simply let Dan go right now."

My mouth opens and out comes a little noise of surprise. "Really?" Firing him hadn't been in my mind.

"Yes, really." Peter is in full on general manager mode. "And whichever you choose, it's entirely your choice. You have the right to decide."

"Uh huh, uh huh," I made noises to fill the space as I mulled this over. I knew I would never say that I wanted Midwest to fire Dan. It didn't warrant it. Did it? Would the consequences of suddenly losing your job be too severe for the crime? I imagined what Dan felt over having his future employment status up in the air, waiting for someone to wave her hand and decide his fate. Waiting for me to decide his fate.

It felt powerful, but an ugly kind of power.

"I know he feels very bad about what he said," Peter said. This didn't come off as dismissive, for I had been thinking the same thing. I imagined, hoped, that given the chain of events that had occurred since Dan's comment, that he had been slapped with shock at the severity of it. That the severity of it might indicate how much it had fucking upset me. How fucked up it was, is, is still. I felt uncomfortable with the power I was suddenly holding, god-like, with the next words to come out of my mouth, but I was pleased that maybe he was sweating bullets over the whole fucking thing. He had, I knew, a teenage daughter. I had seen her, dropping by a jobsite to bring her dad lunch. What had gotten into him that day?

"I don't think he needs to be fired." And I didn't. "Training is fine. I wonder, I wonder if they'll just send him, or the other pump operators too." I wondered if the other guys I saw every week would find out, if they already knew.

Peter agreed. "Are you sure? I want you to be comfortable with the decision."

"Yeah, I am. Firing seems too much. Like I said, I've never had trouble with him before. He's not constantly saying things. That would be different."

A one-time mistake. Are we all allowed that? Of course not. I wondered about the outcome if I had fucked up so grandly and said something I shouldn't have to a customer.

And so it was settled. "You know Linda," Peter said, "we're pretty lucky. Twenty or thirty years ago, for someone like you or I, something like this probably would have been swept under the rug."

"It still gets swept under the rug, Peter." There was no hesitation on this, from me. If he thought all Black men and all women were listened to, believed, taken seriously, his privilege was astounding.

He was silent for a long moment. "You're probably right." No probably, I knew I was.

And now, I ask myself what that really means—to sweep something under the rug. Am I lucky, as Peter said, to work for a company that takes sexual harassment seriously? I suppose I am, considering so many people are denied that right. I felt cared about, but—.

None of those consequences happened because my body, my mind, my inner Linda were cared about, truly. The consequences happened because Midnight and Midwest had jobs to do. After all, no one likes a lawsuit.

I had gone to Lenny, Howard, and Chip out of a desire to be heard, and to poke a hole in this "man's world" and let in someone else's perspective. To expose what I was forced to grapple with. What I had inadvertently done, naively, but not wrongly, was begin a chain of events that Midnight was legally obligated to act on. Without knowing I was doing it, I had lodged a formal complaint of sexual harassment, a dangerous thing for any employer.

Yeah, so, it wasn't swept under the rug on either end. But real paper letters and formal training completed (was it? No one has ever followed up with me), what did any of that really mean? Behind the happy face, the high vis, the sunny smile and bright voice, what toll was exacted for "working through" another aggressive act? Had we moved an inch toward caring more for one another, toward really caring outside business as usual, about what another body and mind endures?

# Refuge

I did the bulk of my graduate student work in a mixer truck. Between you and me and 138.

I read the books on my exam lists in my truck, whenever there was a spare minute. I'd read articles for classes, highlighting passages at 5:00 a.m. in the overhead light of my truck cab. I did homework sitting in the Laforte breakroom with a laptop and a Spanish textbook, guys looking over my shoulder as we argued whether what that Railtown driver said on the radio Friday was racist. I wrote large chunks of my dissertation in 138, struggling to simultaneously balance the laptop and the book I was trying to quote. I will always know what books I've read in the truck, the pencil underlinings a string of wavy undulations from the vibration of the steering wheel as we idled in the parking lot on slow winter days.

 A few months before graduation I sit, thinking again about books that reflect my experience. It is just after 8:00 a.m. and I sit in 138, steering wheel titled up as high as it can go to make space for the computer on my lap. It is minus one degree outside with a windchill of minus twenty-one, and I sit here and wait, hoping not to have a load today, hoping to be told I can go home soon. And yet, the truck is one of the best places to write. Unlike my little house, it is relatively free from distraction, and although it would be misleading to describe the truck's engine with the stereotypical *purrrrr*, it does growl quietly, and the vibration coming through the cab is gentle, and it is quite warm in here.

I sit, waiting to see where my thoughts will take my writing. I ask myself again if I see myself in the books I have encountered throughout my graduate education. Barely, rarely. Just as I often cannot see myself reflected in the trucking world around me, I cannot see myself in these books. I am by and large alone. I feel alone. It is true that I have found bits and pieces of my experience in books, collected scraps of recognition here and there; perhaps this is how many people feel. Or maybe it isn't. Why, I wonder, am I trying to find a reflection of myself somewhere?

I try to think honestly and critically about whether all this is enough, this haphazard way of making connections between my work self and my school self, whether I am searching in the right places. If it is not enough, then what am I expecting, what I should do? Should I be the one to start a "Literature of Labor" course at my university? What if I want to walk away from that world? Would that be giving up, leaving others after me to relive this struggle anew?

I am tempted to stay in this truck cab forever. I am here now because I cannot live without it, not now anyway. I do sometimes wonder what it *would* be like to stay here forever. A part of me would be satisfied to have my only job be trucking, but a piece of me would be missing. Or would I be okay? No. I know without doubt that I'd be unhappy if I left physical labor forever, stationed in an office somewhere, even if it was a nice office with tenure.

I don't know how to combine my two lives. Each of them is a risk. To choose either means hiding part of myself away. Linda

Hogan writes, "I tell parts of my stories here because I have often searched out other lives similar to my own. They would have sustained me. Telling our lives is important, for those who come after us, for those who will see our experience as part of their own historical struggle." I like to see these words on the page. It feels like Hogan is speaking right to me, confirming that I am not alone in my desire to find not just echoes of my story and my life, but a community. Hogan calls us to act outward. To share our stories to help others who are struggling.

If I choose one or the other, driver or academic, then I choose only one half of myself, and who would that person be? What story would be left to tell? I am in this truck now because this life and these people sustain me and make my other work possible. The university gives me a place to tell my stories and enhances the tools I already possess to critically view this world around me. It too gives me life. Hogan writes that her ability to recognize and analyze the daily assaults of classism and racism is what has kept her from losing herself:

> It is sometimes easier to stay where we are, where we know our place, can breathe, know the language, but for the fact that we are largely powerless there to make any change for ourselves, for others, for our children. It is difficult for us to gather our human forces together because our circumstances force us into divisions and anger and self-destruction.

It would be easy to stay in one place or the other; it is much more difficult for me to be in both. Hogan answers the question: why do people search for themselves in the stories of others? They are looking for that human force, to hold *themselves* together, to sustain. To know that there is a place, even if it only exists within the stories of others, where we do not have to choose.

•

As I neared the end of graduate school, I had an easy out for avoiding my future life, the giant "next step" that comes with the achievement of a major milestone like a degree. I was already working at Midnight, and so I could just keep working.

But I was also forced to confront my future because damn if people didn't keep asking me what I wanted to do next. They still do. And I'm not even talking about within the university. My world consisted of truck drivers and concrete guys, who knew I was going to school, and so naturally some of them wondered what someone with a PhD was doing driving a truck. Their question, not mine.

It is an understandable question. I had worked really hard for a big thing. I have a PhD, something that entitles me to a lot, job-wise, no matter your opinion of academia. I couldn't blame people for wanting to know why I was still showing up at Midnight every day. I realized that other people looked at my job as something I did for money, where I looked at it as something that kept me going in more ways than just the financial. I had people at Midnight, and it was an environment that forced me to become a different person, one I liked more than the person I would have been without it.

Skeptics posited that I might just be comfortable. You know, like why one might stay in a less-than-great relationship; you get comfortable, and ending things, starting over, would take so much energy and time and bravery. So, they said, maybe I was just *comfortable*.

But as graduation approached and I thought about my future in the working world, I realized my inertia was about more than where I felt comfortable. I realized how much I had changed from when I began my PhD, and that I no longer wanted the same things, and that what would have satisfied me five years ago would no longer satisfy me. I had my own good reasons for staying, and they didn't include complacency.

# EPILOGUE

# Why I Write

It's a cold and sunny day in December as I write the "end" to this book. I've been racking my brain to figure out how it really ends when of course, we all keep going on, the world keeps spinning, buildings spring up and new roads get paved, students trod in and out of class, doing what they've been told they're supposed to do. I write now where I do most of my thinking, where I *am* the most: at work. Arriving at the jobsite for the university stadium expansion, the customer informs me that it's gonna be awhile, so I retrieve my notebook from the truck cab, lean on the fender of 138, and write. This is a less than ideal place, parked only four feet away from a long string of porta-potties, to which a constant stream of men parade in and out, plastic doors slamming every few minutes as they eye me shyly or don't see me at all, evidence of their bodies wafting toward me, impossible to ignore.

Today has been a pretty good day so far, tomorrow might be a great one, or it could be shit. Part of what causes these swings is external, an environment I'll never control. Part of it is internal, and how do I control that? I don't have answers, but I know there are two things that make me feel *okay*, driving this monster and talking to my guys: releasing the monsters, working through them. Both these things are powerful.

There are three guys pushing wheelbarrows on this job and one of them is real chatty, smiling and super polite but asking me all the expected questions that exhaust me, that I must will myself to answer, again. So today I counter back. How long have you been doing this? How long have *you* been doing it? What did you do before this? It's a long story: what did *you* do? Do you have kids. Sigh. *No.* That was a quick no, he replies, and I ask him why I should have any kids while secretly hoping this book somehow ends up in his hands.

Each time they push a wheelbarrow away, I lean and write. When they return, I set down my pen, fill the wheelbarrow. No one asks me what I am doing, what I write.

My communities might not "get me" the way I need, not all the time. Not most of the time. Those walls are so thick. But I think my voice helps. I have to believe it does. Maybe it matters less that they ask what's with the notebook than that they just, simply, see me here. Long braid, soft voice, standing with my hip out, at ease with 138.

Most days I forget I have a PhD and when I remember, I feel weird. Like I am letting something slip from my hands. Like a dropout, although I haven't. I ever so briefly wonder if it wasn't a stupid mistake not to go on the academic job market before I shove that worry out of mind. That's not who I am, and that's okay.

Something else is out there, is here.

•

A movement in my driver's side mirror catches my eye, and I look to see Ratt barreling across the parking lot. His glasses darken to block the sun, his grin shows the gap in his front teeth. I crank my window down.

"Hey!" Ratt's head appears in full view as he climbs up my cab steps. "Hey, I'm supposed to tell that skinny girl that she did a great job on Friday!" Mateen has nicknamed Ratt "CNN" because he always has the news, and I can see the pleasure in his smile now at having a message to deliver.

I look at him, brows furrowed. What did I even do on Friday? "From who?" I ask.

"The old man Herb, Herb Potter."

Ah! That was it. "So you were at Tom Potter today then?"

"Yeah, I just came from there. We did the approach, but I wasn't even out of the truck when the old man came running up to me and 'bout grabbed me, pulling me over to that hill on the side of the house." Both hands holding the truck, Ratt swayed gently in the air as he talked. "That was a whopper of a hill," he grinned again.

I felt a little thrill in my chest. Pretty cool to get a compliment from someone who'd been around as long as Herb Potter. And Ratt, for that matter.

"I asked him if he said anything to you," Ratt said. "Like if he told you good job."

I laughed a little. "Naw, not really." I let that sink in. "But I'm happy he's still so excited about it today."

We keep talking and I see Chip emerge from goodness knows where, a small notebook cupped in his palm. He drags his feet over to Ratt and me and stands there next to 138. We stop talking and turn our heads to him.

"1:30 a.m. start time Wednesday, are you down?" He stares at us expectantly.

I see Ratt deflate. My sunny mood instantly clouds, thinking about having to rise before midnight. I know what's coming, the sly bitterness about to wash over me, angry how anyone can take a thing I love like driving and wrench the life out of it—

I look at Ratt. He's not swaying now, just hanging on. "Yeah," he mumbles. Chip's question is just a formality.

Chip looks at me and I nod my head in assent. My smile is gone. Chip trips away, off to find the next unsuspecting driver, and Ratt and I are left there together, quiet, suddenly tired.

"Well," he says, the words rolling out like gravel, "I don't know if I can do this much longer. I'm almost 65."

I reach across the steering wheel and give Ratt's shoulder a quick pat. "I know buddy. It's getting really old. We should all just say 'no.'"

His laugh, quick and tight, tells me how possible he thinks that really is. We're both gonna show at 1:30 a.m. the day after tomorrow, driving to work down empty streets, glimpses of hi-vis in a dark parking lot, trucks grumbling to life with as much reluctance as their drivers, still so far from dawn.

It's time for a break.

# Acknowledgments

This book is for my fellow drivers and construction workers. I'm indebted to you for the conversations and the laughs and the struggles we've shared. This book wouldn't have been a thing had it not been for the way you've helped shape my thoughts. My love and special thanks to Nzar Tahir, Glenn White, Rick Straw, Jesus Espinoza Barrera, and David Kochlavashvili (little brother!). Thanks to Jerad Little for taking my favorite trucking picture of me with my beloved 138.

The late Dennis Condon was a dear friend and teacher when I was a true rookie. Thank you, Dennis, for the ice cream in Elgin and for all the miles.

I don't know Kat's last name but I hope my thanks find her somehow. If you know Kat from St. Louis, who was a trainer for Werner Enterprises on the Dollar General route, please put this book in her hands. Kat, when I was right out of truck driving school you were exactly the trainer I needed. You are patient and funny and kind. My memory frequently reaches back to you; I am so grateful for the kindness and the knowledge you shared with me. And for the space! That Freightliner sleeper was your home away from home and you shared it with awkward, moody me.

My English professors at the University of Nebraska Omaha were my earliest champions. Bob Darcy and Chuck Joanningsmeier were instrumental during my BA days, encouraging and patient and generous with advice. John Price, Lisa Knopp, and John McKenna were the mentors I needed to start (and keep going on!) my writing journey. I'll always be in debt to the wonderful David Peterson for his generosity, wisdom, and letting me know that yes, indeed, even trucking is a text, and I can write about it.

My guides and mentors at the University of Nebraska Lincoln are a badass group of women that got me through and taught me a lot about strength along the way. Thank you to Amelia María de la Luz Montes, Joy Castro, Melissa Homestead, Julia Schleck, Maureen Honey, and Ingrid Robyn. Muchísimas gracias to Luis Othoniel Rosa for putting a life-changing book in my hands. And to a rare bird and role model who let me cultivate the trucking thing—thanks a million Tom Gannon. I wish I'd found your classes earlier!

My gratitude to Kristen Elias Rowley, Samara Rafert, and the fabulous team at Mad Creek Books. It's been an exciting process, and I'm fortunate to have you steering the ship!

Jaime, Estabas allí mientras se desarrollaban las historias que se convirtieron en este libro. Me has enseñado español pero también sobre el trabajo de concreto plano y muchas otras cosas. Y luego estaban los viajes por carretera con Trucktuga. Muchas gracias maestro.

Bpaw, what can I say? Thanks again for the check and for being my amazing dad. Thanks mom, for your steadfast enthusiasm and excitement, and to Jason, because you're my brother, and that's enough. Thank you, Bob Finley, for helping me see this thing through.

To Agatha and dear, sweet Alice. My best girls. We miss you Al.

# Notes

## SOME CRAZY TOM POTTER SHIT

**his nose pointed at the bottom:** There is a long-standing tradition of boats, cars, trucks, and other machines being named and referred to in the feminine, primarily by men. I do not know how or when this tradition started; perhaps long-ago homesick sailors christened their ships with the names of those they pined for. To me, the feminization of machines is another way of objectifying women; for this reason, as a small form of resistance, my trucks are always "he."

## NAVIGATING

**And yet living with a border running underneath me:** For more about borders and borderlands theory, see Gloria Anzaldúa's *Borderlands/La Frontera: The New Mestiza*.

**I have a knapsack full of privileges:** For more on the idea of a "privilege knapsack," see Peggy McIntosh, "White Privilege and Male Privilege: A Personal Account of Coming to See

Correspondences through Work in Women's Studies," in *Race, Class, and Gender: An Anthology*, 4th edition.

## DEFINITIONS

**I use *work* here in the way:** See Mike Rose, *The Mind at Work: Valuing the Intelligence of the American Worker*.

## CITE YOUR WORK

**When I say that I spent my life:** Read Linda Hogan, "The Two Lives," in *I Tell You Now: Autobiographical Essays by Native American Writers*. All the material I quote from Hogan comes from this essay.

## A TRUCK DRIVER IS BORN

**Because I wanted to—I became a trucker:** "Rookie Run." *Ice Road Truckers*, season 3, episode 2.
**I already have a CDL:** A CDL is a commercial driver's license.

## MY PRETTY EYES

**Fifty years ago, film theorist Laura Mulvey:** See Laura Mulvey's "Visual Pleasure and Narrative Cinema," originally published in 1975, and collected in *Issues in Feminist Film Criticism*, edited by Patricia Erens, 1990.

# AND YET ANOTHER INSTANCE WHERE A WORD WIELDS ITS POWER

**like marbles in the mouth:** This phrase comes from Daisy Hernández, *A Cup of Water Under My Bed.*
**a border tongue, a forked tongue:** Gloria Anzaldúa, *Borderlands/La Frontera: The New Mestiza*

# LEGAL PROTECTION

**So much for what Marx termed** and **What you don't necessarily realize:** Barbara Ehrenreich, *Nickel and Dimed: On (Not) Getting by in America.* All material I quote from Ehrenreich comes from this text.
**Eight hours for work, eight hours:** David R. Roediger and Philip S. Foner, *Our Own Time: A History of American Labor and the Working Day.*
**Work . . . has no feelings:** Sarah Jaffe, *Work Won't Love You Back: How Devotion to Our Jobs Keeps Us Exploited, Exhausted, and Alone.*

# ASSETS

**Anybody who is experiencing something:** Gloria Steinem, *My Life on the Road.*
**You guys are our biggest assets:** My fight over the use of the blanket term "guys" to refer to a group of people who are not all "guys" is another discussion, one that I have had with both Steven and Betty. Neither of them has gone beyond half-hearted attempts to change their language, despite my suggestions of using "you," or "you all." I

want to give credit to John Leonard Harris, a Lincoln-based encouragement consultant and speaker who spoke to Midnight employees in February of 2022, for easily solving the problem of inclusion by referring to our group (where I was the only woman in a room of about fifty people) as "brothers and sisters" or simply "friends."

**The university is a place where middle managers:** See Samuel Bowles and Herbert Gintis, *Schooling in Capitalist America: Educational Reform and the Contradictions of Economic Life.*

**Women with peculiar bleached yellow faces** and **You can tell a weaver by the skin:** See Elizabeth Stuart Phelps, *The Silent Partner.*

**During my first four years working in construction:** "Authorities identify construction worker killed in Lincoln accident," *6 News WOWT,* 23 Dec. 2019, and "UPDATE: Police identify individual killed due to Friday's construction accident at CEDARS," *1011 NOW,* 3 Jan. 2021.

**And there are the social markers:** For more on social responses to uniforms and what uniforms allow workers (or don't), see the episode "Uniform," *Worn Stories,* on Netflix.

**Then there's the supermarket:** Barbara Ehrenreich, *Nickel and Dimed.*

## ¿PERO DÓNDE ESTÁN LOS HISPANOS?

**They always tell stories we already know:** *Martin Eden.* Directed by Pietro Marcello.

**The news story itself is titled:** For all quoted material from the news story, see Abbie Petersen, "Missing Cat Found in Home's Foundation." *1011 NOW.* KOLN, 9 Dec. 2019.

**I felt like calling out:** About a month prior to the first draft of this moment, I was walking through the first floor of Andrews

Hall on my way to Burnett Hall for my Spanish class. Two facilities employees were pushing a small machine through the hallway. Dressed in casual student clothes, I waited to hold open the door for them. The older man looked at me, paused, then exclaimed, "Concrete girl!" I grinned, caught completely off guard. It was a delightful moment. I can only assume he has seen me as he has driven by our plant, though I'm still quite surprised at his recognition.

## SCHOOLED

**Low-wage workers are no more homogeneous:** Barbara Ehrenreich, *Nickel and Dimed*.
**The university graduate has been schooled** and **Everywhere, all children know:** Ivan Illich, *Deschooling Society*.

## CRAFT

**And oh, operating it:** For a detailed look at the high-level of skills and cognitive acts it takes to perform working-class jobs that historically might be considered as craft-less, skill-less, or as simply *less*, see Mike Rose, *The Mind at Work: Valuing the Intelligence of the American Worker*.

## WHAT WE MIGHT DO

**the whole orderly conduct of life:** This phrase comes directly from Andreas Malm's *How to Blow Up a Pipeline*.

## UNIFORM

**the hopper of the pump truck:** A concrete pump truck is a vehicle equipped with a hopper at its back end into which concrete mixers can unload. A valve system sucks concrete from the hopper into pipe connected to a boom. The boom can be unfolded from the pump truck and can reach vertically and horizontally across a great distance (on average, up to 140 feet) where concrete leaves the pipe via a hose attached to the end. The pump truck's reach allows concrete to be easily placed where mixer trucks can't get to, for example, into a hole with footings, inside buildings, or up onto "decks," the newly constructed floors of multifloor buildings.

**although we've had our awkward moments:** A few weeks into my Midnight career, Tony, whose name I didn't know at the time and with whom I had barely interacted, commented that I was "his favorite driver." It was clear from the context that this favoritism had nothing to do with my excellent driving skills, and long afterward I loathed to go to a job where I knew I'd see him. Perhaps a year later, at a particularly slow and agonizingly boring job pumping concrete for a pool, Tony told me he didn't mind the slowness because "he got to stand here and look at a super-hot chick all day," meaning, apparently, me. I told him quite seriously that his words weren't professionally appropriate, to which his eyes grew wide before he apologized. Since then, he's never said anything unprofessional, and has proved to be one of the most enjoyable and trustworthy pump operators to work with.

## OUT OF PLACE

**he says in Spanish:** Unless otherwise noted, this conversation took place in Spanish.

## LACKING

**notwithstanding the three women:** The History Channel added two more women to the cast lineup in seasons five and ten; notably, like Kelly, they are young and conform to mainstream white female beauty standards.

**A lone woman is one thing:** As Land frequently notes throughout *Maid*, single mothers are constantly judged and ostracized, viewed as irresponsible failures for their procreation without participation in a larger family unit. Poor single mothers experience still more judgement and discrimination.

## TALKING BACK

**When listeners hear a female voice** and **how women were and are allowed to speak:** See (and hear) Mary Beard, *Women & Power: A Manifesto*.

# Further Reading

There are many books and essays that have been indispensable to me for thinking about class, labor, and schooling. In addition to the works I've quoted and the texts listed in the "Notes" section of this book, please see the following list for my recommendations for further reading.

*The Big Rig: Trucking and the Decline of the American Dream,* by Steve Viscelli
*Chicana Without Apology: The New Chicana Cultural Studies,* by Edén Torres
"Chicanismo, DuBois, and Double-Consciousness," by Dominic Saucedo
*Dirt Work: An Education in the Woods,* by Christine Byl
*Educated,* by Tara Westover
*Gray Areas: How the Way We Work Perpetuates Racism and What We Can Do to Fix It,* by Adia Harvey Wingfield
*If Schools Didn't Exist: A Study in the Sociology of Schools,* by Nils Christie
*Island of Bones: Essays,* by Joy Castro
*Make Your Home Among Strangers,* by Jennine Capó Crucet
*My Time Among the Whites: Notes from an Unfinished Education,* by Jennine Capó Crucet
*Under the Feet of Jesus,* by Helena María Viramontes
*We'll Call You if We Need You: Experiences of Women Working Construction,* by Susan Eisenberg
*Working,* by Studs Terkel

# MACHETE
## Joy Castro and Rachel Cochran, Series Editors

This series showcases fresh stories, innovative forms, and books that break new aesthetic ground in nonfiction—memoir, personal and lyric essay, literary journalism, cultural meditations, short shorts, hybrid essays, graphic pieces, and more—from authors whose writing has historically been marginalized, ignored, and passed over. The series is explicitly interested in not only ethnic and racial diversity, but also gender and sexual diversity, neurodiversity, physical diversity, religious diversity, cultural diversity, and diversity in all of its manifestations. The machete enables path-clearing; it hacks new trails and carves out new directions. The Machete series celebrates and shepherds unique new voices into publication, providing a platform for writers whose work intervenes in dangerous ways.

*Clutch*
LINDA PAWLENTY

*Women Surrounded by Water: A Memoir*
PATRICIA CORAL

*I Would Meet You Anywhere: A Memoir*
SUSAN KIYO ITO

*Birding While Indian: A Mixed-Blood Memoir*
THOMAS C. GANNON

*Chi Boy: Native Sons and Chicago Reckonings*
KEENAN NORRIS

*We Take Our Cities with Us: A Memoir*
SORAYYA KHAN

*The Sound of Memory: Themes from a Violinist's Life*
REBECCA FISCHER

*Finding Querencia: Essays from In-Between*
HARRISON CANDELARIA FLETCHER

*Eating Lightbulbs and Other Essays*
STEVE FELLNER

*The Guild of the Infant Saviour: An Adopted Child's Memory Book*
MEGAN CULHANE GALBRAITH

*Like Love*
MICHELE MORANO

*Quite Mad: An American Pharma Memoir*
SARAH FAWN MONTGOMERY

*Apocalypse, Darling*
BARRIE JEAN BORICH

www.ingramcontent.com/pod-product-compliance
Lightning Source LLC
Chambersburg PA
CBHW021349280525
27334CB00003B/121